CW00857672

Titles in the 'Women *Plus*' series:

Talented women

Edited by

Jocelyne Étienne-Nugue

UNESCO PUBLISHING · Women *plus*

Photo credits
pp. 17, 103, 106: Victor France; p. 19: Nalda Searles;
p. 20 (bottom): John Austin; pp. 27, 29: Claudia
Aseneth Montero; p. 31: Claudia Uribe; pp. 35, 39, 40,
42: Shalini Saran; p. 47: Niall McInerney; pp. 51, 52:
Eugène Langan; pp. 63, 66, 68: Racine Keita; pp. 73,
74, 78: Jasleen Dhamija; pp. 83, 85, 86: Abdelaziz
Frikha; pp. 93, 94, 96: Caroline Ramsay.

The ideas and opinions expressed in this work are those
of the authors and do not necessarily represent the views
of UNESCO.

This book has been realized by several hands at the
initiative of the Division of Arts and Cultural Life of
UNESCO.

Published in 1995 by the
United Nations Educational,
Scientific and Cultural Organization,
7, place de Fontenoy,
75352 Paris 07 SP

Graphic design by J.-F. Chériez
Layout by Susanne Almeida-Klein
Maps by Ewa Maruszewska
Printed by Marco Gráfico, Madrid (Spain)

ISBN 92-3-103201-1

© UNESCO 1995

Preface

In many societies throughout the world, it is mainly women who have possessed, handed down and transformed craft skills. They have created new forms and new combinations of materials and techniques, thereby giving birth to original objects combining utilitarian and aesthetic features, and demonstrating that arts and crafts involve more than the mere reproduction of ancestral techniques as they embody one of the privileged domains of feminine creativity.

It has also been in this so-called 'informal' sector, lying between the economic and cultural fields, that craftswomen, particularly in underprivileged countries and areas, have most successfully displayed the qualities of responsible citizenship. But at what cost! The obstacles they have had to overcome to secure rightful recognition of their talents, their work and their role in society are all too often the reflection and result of persisting inequality.

In 1995, the year of the Fourth World Conference on Women, we believe that it is important to proclaim the major role that women play in the economic, social and cultural development of society and, what is more, to reveal it quite unequivocally. By publishing accounts of the experience of craftswomen from the five continents in regard to their approach to life, their difficulties and their aspirations, UNESCO seeks to draw the attention of the international community and decision-makers to the need to enhance women's capacities and experience. The purpose of this work is not merely to pay tribute to the inventiveness and energy of craftswomen in their struggle to create enterprises and derive an income that can enable them to sustain their families. It is, above all, an eloquent illustration of the wealth of human talent of which women are the custodians and that deserves to be more widely known so as to be recognized, enhanced and made to fructify for the greater welfare of all.

Federico Mayor
Director-General
of UNESCO

Contents

Introduction

Regardless of the country they belong to, women have always played a vital role in safeguarding traditions and in passing on the rules of conduct and the skills which they believe indispensable in maintaining the cohesion of the family and a place in society. Through their intuition and sensitivity, they have also known, better than anyone else, how to adapt and then refashion them in accordance with the process of change and progress that has left its mark on humankind through the course of time.

In the active and eminently competitive world of today, women have managed to find a place for themselves, often in the very forefront, but have had the wisdom to remain profoundly attached to traditional patterns of reference that have provided them with reassurance and greater fulfilment. In the fields of art, manual skills and particularly arts and crafts, it is interesting to observe how their success has been linked to simple methods and practices and a return to those resources that they know to be ancient yet precious, in such a way as to incorporate them in an innovative approach.

It is not by coincidence that UNESCO has now taken the initiative of inviting a number of these women to relate their experience. By their presence and the part they play in the creative field of arts and crafts, women, just like men, have always featured in the numerous actions conducted by the Division of Arts and Cultural Life on behalf of 'innovative craftspeople in the world'. Whether it be for the Prize for Creativity, awarded several times to craftswomen, or among contemporary creations presented at the leading Salons de Décoration, or at thematic exhibitions organized on the occasion of the General Conference of UNESCO or within research and creation workshops organized in various countries, women's inventiveness and talent have been recognized and celebrated for their indisputable value.

The time has come for them to speak out about their feminine creativity with its pitfalls and its rewards.

Women speak up

Craftswomen here relate the lives they lead and their desire to create, and the skills that have been handed down to them via many generations and which they would dearly like to maintain and sustain and then pass on to the inventive hands of their daughters.

They also reveal their dissatisfaction and the feeling they often have of being underconsidered, underemployed and undervalued in the society to which they belong and where they are condemned to working at home, bound as they are by conflicting activities, making demands on their time that are never taken into account. They tell us of their aspirations for a fairer, better recognized position in society and for self-fulfilment without fear or limitation. There is nothing new here but we are once again made aware that in many parts of the world, in spite of progress achieved over more than a century, much has still to be done for these craftswomen whom the more privileged have yet to listen to, accompany and help so that they may truly fulfil that ever-hidden facet of themselves, namely, their ability to create.

Quite calmly and without bitterness, various creative women relate the unswerving path they have followed for so long towards deserved professional recognition. Separated by continents and oceans, they come from worlds so different that it is surprising to see how close in fact they are to each other, even if most of them share the fate of living far from the major capitals, in rural areas that are isolated and often underprivileged.

Joined fortunes

What is the subtle link that binds them?

Whether they be from Africa, Australia, Colombia, India or Thailand, their lives are similar. Mostly of rural, though sometimes urban origin, they are all creators or entrepreneurs, wives and mothers. Some work and struggle alone while others pool their efforts in order to fight more effectively. What is most striking, however, is that each of them possesses those fundamental qualities that sustain life; each of them copes, using the means at her disposal, with the problems that arise and each of them remains attentive to others and to the world around her.

Regardless of their origins, these women have always succeeded in preserving

fundamental gestures, recovering them, adapting them and renewing them so that the fundamental pattern of life may go on, regardless. They have ensured a degree of 'permanence' and maintained some continuity in life by linking the past with the present, daily experience with that of dreams, the ordinary with the sublime and the useful with the artistic.

Women's hands are the privileged instruments of daily, creative gestures. They symbolize both agility and efficacity as well as gentleness and beauty. Instruments of combat as well as instruments of happiness, they are mobile, active, adroit, firm or tender, never at rest from childhood onwards, busy kneading, sewing, plaiting, changing and rocking their children, weaving, combing, dressing and stroking . . . they know where to find paths, how to invent methods for taming nature and the environment, however hostile.

Through their craftswomen's hands, they show with their talents the desire to win for themselves what society has been slow in giving them; they make their presence felt and assert their rights and gradually sustain their culture and identity.

This underlines the arduous but resolute paths that such artists as Sadika from Tunisia and Mel from Ireland have followed, both magicians in their fields of glass-blowing and silk-painting. It is with the same serenity that Ramrati in India and M'athabo in Lesotho fashion clay according to traditional methods under their children's attentive eye. It is with the conviction of preserving the talents peculiar to her own people that Khun Na has passed on to her daughter the secrets of Thai silk *ikat* and in order to assert the originality of her culture that Aminata encourages the craftspeople of Mali to work for foreign orders. In like wise, Gabriella, Adelfa and other Embera women in Colombia seek to

10

exercise decision-making power in community and family life by establishing links with the outside world while acquiring purchasing power. And elsewhere, Nalda in Australia, Carolyn in the United States and Rufina in Uruguay, by their awareness and energy, have encouraged less fortunate craftspeople to work together more productively.

All the women described here have succeeded in achieving fulfilment through traditional techniques which they have managed to adapt to the requirements of contemporary society and have thus shown that, as neglected partners in the community, they are still part of the contemporary scene and work in symbiosis with their times. Their meticulous research, sense of perfection and profound intuition for true beauty have enabled them to become leading artists, recognized, admired and more prosperous but at the expense of tireless personal effort and a life that is both twofold and dual as they have never, at any time, been able to separate their creative activities from their domestic responsibilities.

We shall observe them working, living and struggling. They love what they do and want to continue doing it, and in the way they please. It is through their tireless, industrious gestures that they have made things change. Irreversibly.

The experience of these women proves, if that was still necessary, that it is in the field of education, training, minimal material help and straightforward encouragement that they most urgently require support. They could then devote themselves more fully to creation and innovation.

In Africa, Asia and Latin America, countrywomen are craftswomen by tradition and by necessity. Many are talented artists without being aware of it, perpetuating skills handed down to them from earlier generations, from mother to daughter, merely to satisfy family needs and provide a modest personal income. Very few of them succeed in going beyond that.

The case of M'athabo, an inventive but unschooled potter in the tiny state of Lesotho, lying in the heart of South Africa, and the case of Ramrati, in a potters' hamlet on the outskirts of Delhi, are by no means unique but continue to be rare even if the curiosity of tourists, collectors and tradesmen has succeeded in bringing out of anonymity works that are appreciated for their quality and originality in distant lands.

There is also the hut painted by Esther Mahlangu, a South African woman, revealed at the 'Magicians of the Earth' exhibition in Paris (1989) and the eccentric characters of the Senegalese potter, Seni Camara, to be found in museums today after having been sold in the market of Casamance.

The taste for ethnic designs has furnished shops and galleries throughout the world with objects and textiles created by anonymous craftswomen too isolated or powerless to claim their share of success and derive any economic benefit. If only we could remember the names and faces of the women in small Malian villages along the Niger who, with such precision and mastery, draw the contrasted symbols of the *bogolans* that have come to be so sought after by decorators and stylists in the capitals of rich countries.

In the cities, the women who are more active and more familiar with trends in fashion and trade have succeeded in making themselves heard more effectively. They are better equipped, better trained and more audacious. But will they succeed in remaining creative to the degree they want or will they inevitably become businesswomen, first and foremost? Aissa Dione, a textile stylist in Dakar, and Oumou Sangho, a jewellery designer in Côte d'Ivoire, both of whom have been awarded the UNESCO Prize for Arts and Crafts, together with Kong Thong, a silk-weaver in Laos, could also have much to say about their recent experience and the success of their products that have made them organize their lives differently in economic terms.

In a different context, the case of Mel Bradley, an Irishwoman from Dublin who graduated from an Institute of Art and Design but would like to remain a sensitive craftswoman, free to organize her career as she wishes, illustrates how difficult it is for an isolated artist to strike a balance between professional success and a choice of lifestyle. Only her tireless determination and the certitude of her objectives have enabled her to overcome the usual obstacles, such as fatigue from compulsory travel, difficult managerial tasks without support and the rigour of working to a deadline, to be reconciled with the attention she would like to give to her son and her husband and her desire to decorate their home! She too thinks that governments ought to do more to stimulate and make use of women's energy and experience.

Like Mel, Sadika who set up a workshop on the attractive outskirts of Tunis where she could work as she liked and initiate young apprentices to the art of glass-making, has followed a path both comparable and exemplary in its choices, battles and personal success: 'I can now reconcile my life as an artist and craftswoman and my family commitments . . . but I had to wait eight years before obtaining authorization to open my workshop in the Gammarth district'. Nobody seemed to have any faith in this success which today is a credit to Tunisia. Nevertheless, women's crafts in that country (weaving, embroidery and plaiting), whether in rural or urban areas, have long been encouraged and

supported by government through the National Arts and Crafts Board. Such support, however, has almost always been directed towards family or corporate enterprises in which various talents are combined in a joint production process that becomes an integral part of the national economy.

Creating together

In most countries, associations and co-operatives are an efficient process for enabling craftspeople, whether men or women, to contribute to economic development. When they come together in groups, women know that they can defend their interests more effectively by sharing out tasks and responsibilities according to their various skills. The more educated and dynamic then tackle problems relating to organization, training and development on behalf of the group as a whole.

This is precisely what has taken place in Australia thanks to the endeavours of Nalda Searles – a sculptor of fibres rather than basketry – among aboriginal women in her area who have admirable skills in plaiting vegetable matter and whose traditional crafts she has revived. By helping them in their work and guiding their creation, she has enabled them to gain access to national and international markets and obtain the support of local financial bodies.

It is indisputable that interest shown in the aboriginal arts since the 1960s has facilitated this approach and provided a basis for a favourable welcome, after the immense success of woven fibres and paintings on wood or bark in the Arnhem land, for the modest works, but remarkable by their finesse and inventiveness, of the basket-weavers of the less familiar communities of Western Australia, as well as for the works they inspire.

A similarly decisive role has been played

by Carolyn McKecuen, an American craftswoman from North Carolina who developed a small co-operative into an organization with a major trade mark in order to make use of, perfect and distribute the work of all those craftswomen who had hitherto been penalized by their isolation in the south-eastern rural areas of the United States. This organization has achieved outstanding success in economic and human terms with annual sales amounting to $600,000 and has just been selected by the Co-operative Fund for the Economic Development of Women.

This initiative, though undoubtedly the most edifying, has not been unique in the United States. This continent, invariably a symbol of progress, has always shown great interest in craftspeople and their techniques, whether the most ancient or most modern, through museums, galleries and publications (including the long-established magazine, *The Craftsman*) or national events such as 'The Year of American Craft'.

It may also be because they have mastered the most advanced technologies that Americans attach such importance to craft talents which associations, such as the very active 'Aid to Artisans', endeavour to discover and support, both at home and throughout the world.

In Latin America, where arts and crafts have always been of considerable historical and cultural importance, the activity of craftspeople has been sustained over the centuries for fundamental economic reasons. In most states, the government oversees this productive sector through official structures and operational bodies such as Artesanías de Colombia, Fonart in Mexico, Matra in Argentina, Artesanías y Folclor in Venezuela and Manos del Uruguay.

The action and projects supported by these bodies on behalf of craftswomen have been based, more often than not, on co-operative associations, particularly in inland areas where rural craftswomen have found it difficult to set up their own organizations in a context where ignorance and family and social pressures tend to stifle their ambitions and enthusiasm.

Basket-makers in the Andean communities of south-east Colombia have joined together in associations after having worked for a long time within the traditional, family economy where they had no control over the marketing of their products which remained largely a male responsibility. They now constitute one of the most active co-operatives in this area along the Pacific and, thanks to regional programmes funded by the EC and supported by Artesanías de Colombia, have managed to broaden and adapt their skills in order to organize their production more effectively and benefit directly from the proceeds of their work. Various experiments of this kind in Colombia have enabled local craftswomen to become more aware of their shortcomings, as well as their capacities and desire to become involved in the outside world.

There are many similarities to be found in the strategies adopted by Manos del Uruguay to encourage isolated women involved in textile crafts in the inland areas of the country to set up autonomous co-operatives which they manage themselves with the assistance of a central office in the capital. Once again, it was the lucidity and willpower of a particular woman, she too a weaver, but in contact with the urban environment, which enabled this organization to be set up and to offer craftswomen opportunities for further training and encourage their initiatives in creation. The creative spirit can develop at long last and renew itself successfully through co-operation

13

with artists and designers who are now interested in products whose value they truly appreciate. If we bear in mind the figures put forward by one of the Manos officials, referring to 600 craftswomen in 18 co-operatives belonging to 90 groups in 40 localities, it is clear that the members can now make their voices heard and their claims recognized.

We might well wish that approaches such as these serve as an example, particularly in the economically underdeveloped countries that have rich though frequently neglected craft traditions. In Mali, for example, the energy of a talented, cultivated woman such as Aminata Traoré has successfully awakened some consciences, although she is still insufficiently appreciated and supported. By seeking the collaboration of the still numerous craftswomen in the villages and by giving their products worldwide attention, she has attempted to persuade people that these potters and dyers have something worthwhile to say and to pass on. It is through this original cultural venture, which she would like to be all-embracing, as it combines culture, research, art and the culinary tradition, that she chooses to organize the promotion and marketing of a traditional heritage which she knows is also a valuable economic asset.

Women such as Aminata, M'athabo, Sadika, Nalda, Ramrati, Khun Na, Carolyn and Mel, as well as the Emberas in Colombia and the craftswomen of Manos del Uruguay, apart from belonging to Africa, Asia, Europe and America, have revealed the profound qualities they share; inventive, sensitive, sturdy, plucky, patient and generous though

they may be, they are also conscious of being responsible for maintaining a particular type of society and lifestyle.

Through the testimony of their experience, it would seem that while the overall status of women may vary from one country to another or may differ according to social strata, there are major similarities in craftswomen's circumstances throughout the world, particularly in rural areas: their isolation, poverty and exclusion. For many of them, the absence of education has particularly serious consequences as it limits access to relative freedom and the outside world. All have the same desire for professional success and a well-balanced private life without having to sacrifice one for the benefit of the other.

Throughout their experience, they have shown us how they have sought, and often found, the means of overcoming the inevitable obstacles one by one and of achieving success in spite of everything.

In accordance with the wishes of Gertrude Mongella, Secretary-General of the World Conference on Women held in Beijing in September 1995, the meeting hopefully would give 'women throughout the world an opportunity to use the diversity of their origins as a means of combating the subordinate status of women in society'.

It is precisely by breaking out of their isolation and seeking agreement on what they believe to be priority issues that creative women today will find and impose new solutions in order to play a part in the forms of development that concern them.

Jocelyne Étienne-Nugue

14

Nalda Searles:

the language of the landscape

by Helen Ross

Perth   Sydney

16

Most of us in Australia have developed a special relationship with the landscape and the environment through the way we look at them. For Nalda Searles the landscape has always been a source of multiple experience, not that which develops from the visual experience itself but rather that born out of the circumstances of her own life.

The career of this Western Australian woman reflects many aspects of the current circumstances of craftswomen in this part of the world where each day seems to bring new opportunities such as holding exhibitions of their work in public or private galleries, commissioning for public artworks, organizing exhibitions, and teaching and conducting workshops for art students and the general public. Nalda's experience has also included learning from and subsequently helping to revitalize craft practices among aboriginal women.

Nalda was born in 1945 and grew up in a large family in the goldfield town of Kalgoorlie, 500 km inland from Perth. Kalgoorlie stands on the edge of the Central Western Desert and, as a child, Nalda would roam freely in this harsh but complex environment, inventing games and using whatever materials came to hand. Looking back on this period of her life, she feels that 'there is no equivalent cultural experience' to

this freedom and, on account of this background, as a white Australian, she is able to overcome the problem of what she calls 'being illiterate or dumbstruck in the midst of a landscape'. Nalda left school at 15 and trained as an assistant psychiatric nurse and worked in that profession until she was 30, living in Africa and travelling between 1971 and 1975. She then nursed her mother till the latter died in 1977.

At this stage, she felt that her life needed to take a new direction and became interested in photography. She was living with her family in Perth and, one evening, agreed to accompany her sister to a macramé evening class. Macramé was first developed by Arab weavers in the thirteenth century and had become a popular craft among Australian women in the 1970s and 1980s. It is the art of creating practical and decorative objects made from knotted cord, rope or string. This 'playing with string', as Nalda called it, soon became a passion for her.

Her early works were only two-dimensional. It was a process of bringing together different aspects of the landscape by using material gathered from the natural environment, and then woven together with string. The origin of these materials was as important as their appearance; she could tell where every stick came from so that the

NALDA SEARLES
AT HOME
WITH A GRASS
TEA SET.

finished work was like a map woven with material bearing the mark of where it had come from.

By 1982, her interest had focused on basketry, which was influenced by the work of the American Indians. During a four-month trip to the United States, she was also attracted by a wide range of contemporary basketry, particularly the work of Douglas Fuchs. Nalda realized that this three-dimensional technique 'could become an intellectual as well as a creative and a physical exercise – and would thus embrace the whole range of my needs'. The baskets were never made for functional purposes but simply for the pleasure of making, 'the amazement of creation', as she called it.

In 1983, Nalda met a famous Western Australian potter, Eileen Keys, with whom she shared a great love of the harsh Western Australian environment. Her development in the use of nature as a source of inspiration and materials was guided and encouraged by Eileen Keys.

By this time, Nalda had built up a wide reputation through teaching and exhibiting but admits that she was 'shy, lacking in confidence about the value of what I was doing'. She felt it was time to measure herself in an academic environment and so, in 1989, she began a Visual Arts diploma at Curtin University of Technology.

The School of Art within this university has always considered the crafts to be as important as the fine arts and provides specialized workshops in ceramics and glass, textiles and jewellery. This is also the case in many places in Australia. Wherever art is taught at university level, the craft students are expected to have the same aspirations as painters and sculptors; that is to say, they can create original exhibition-standard works of art which often only bear a vague reference to their original technique.

At Art School, Nalda chose to enrol in painting rather than textiles because painting was an area she knew nothing about whereas she already had quite a lot of experience in textiles. As pointed out earlier, the crafts and the fine arts in Australia have much similarity of purpose and, consequently, artists are often involved with a craft and craftspeople often paint.

Nalda graduated from Curtin University in 1991 with a dual diploma in painting and the use of natural materials in art.

Even before graduating, Nalda had begun teaching in the Textiles Department of the Art School at Edith Cowan University. Each year since 1986, she has taken a group of between twenty and fifty students camping in a remote bushland area so that they can become more familiar with the natural environment and discover ways in which they can make art from and with found materials. Little by little, they find ways to use the land as a source of spiritual, visual and material inspiration. Every day, a new technique is taught, such as leaf dyeing, collecting and firing clay, basketry techniques and cord weaving from natural fibres.

Another artist often joins the group of aboriginal women artists to work alongside the students. It is not always easy to find ways in which aboriginal and white Australians can get to know each other. Art is one way in which this link can be established and these camps have become a very valuable way of teaching respect for the natural environment and for aboriginal traditions.

Nalda is a well-known community arts person. In Australia, community arts are seen as an important means of developing a positive community spirit and of providing recreational activities for all age-groups.

Many local councils have a community arts person who runs programmes such as

18

MARY MCLEAN WITH SHOES
MADE OF EMU FEATHERS AND WOOL,
A VARIATION ON
TRADITIONAL CEREMONIAL SLIPPERS.

painting a mural for a public place, puppetry workshops or making banners for local festivals.

In 1991, the Warta Kutju Aboriginal Corporation invited Nalda to conduct a workshop for aboriginal people in Kalgoorlie. It proved a great success and was held again in 1992. The project was funded by Healthway, a funding body for sports and arts projects in Western Australia, thanks to revenue from duty levied on cigarettes. At the second workshop, Nalda met Mary McLean, an aboriginal woman from the Wongutha language group. Mary was known to be a talented sculptress and painter. The two

women became good friends and have since worked on many projects together.

Nalda says that spending time with Mary has meant that she has come to see the landscape in a new light and that she feels more 'at home'. Mary has taught her how to find bush food and berries, to grind seeds and cook bread, emu and goanna meat.

They have learnt something from each other and, under Nalda's influence, Mary has become more confident as a painter and has begun to use more figurative elements in her paintings. She now tells stories about her own life in her paintings and in a very short time has become a well-known artist throughout

20

*ABOVE: BASKET BY NALDA SEARLES
OF LOCAL WICKER AND
EMU FEATHERS.
PEARL HANDLES BY MARY MCLEAN.
RIGHT: LARGE WICKERWORK
CARRYING BASKET (45 × 34 CM)
BY MARY MIRDABURWA.*

Australia. Her paintings are to be found in many state galleries and fetch high prices.

In 1994, Nalda and Mary were invited to teach basketry to a group of Nyungar women at Narrogin, in the south-west of Western Australia. The young women in this town had grown up without access to their traditional crafts which, like most of their culture, had been lost with the destruction of their society in the years following white settlement. Along with Nalda and Mary, the women began making baskets according to the basic coiling method using grasses which were gathered from the old reserves where they still grow. This is a type of grass (*Romula roseata*), commonly called 'Guildford grass', which Marjorie Ridley used to make baskets in Perth in the 1950s. Nalda had done a lot of research on Marjorie Ridley's work and was therefore able to find evidence of how this particular grass had been used in the past. Yet little is known of the traditional customs of the aboriginal people from the south-west. There are a few examples of fish traps woven from fibre, but whether basketry was also produced is not known.

The Narrogin women have been successful in finding markets for their baskets, cord and seed necklaces and also for their rag dolls which they make from recycled clothing. Their craft practice is quite individual as there is no tradition to draw on but as Nalda points out, 'a spirit of creativity, dormant for so long, is now being awakened'.

Another interesting point she makes is that in traditional societies, only a few craft objects were made for their own use, as carved dishes, spears and arrows lasted a long time. Today, the craftswomen produce many more such items than they otherwise would in order to meet demand on national and international markets. For Mary, the pleasure is in the making but she is also happy to sell her work.

A number of organizations provide support for the marketing of aboriginal craftwork and ensure that the craftspeople are paid properly for their work. In remote communities, an arts officer manages the exhibiting and sale of work, and directories listing all of these craft communities and how to contact them are available.

Many aboriginal women exhibit work in galleries and museums. In December 1994, for example, the Fremantle Arts Centre held a major exhibition on 'High Fibre Diet' which included the cultural traditions in present-day Australia, both aboriginal and European. In the catalogue, Nalda Searles wrote: 'Plastic bags have superseded the fibre basket and yet we are still drawn to the feel of grasses, reeds, roots and leaves. We are still drawn to the mystery of their construction into a coherent form. The certainty of the seasons – the knowledge that grass will grow, barks will peel, leaves will grow again – ensures a pattern that cannot be ignored. This is probably why, ephemeral though it is, basketry has been kept alive and its technique has greatly evolved, despite a rather sketchy documented history. In much of aboriginal Australia some of the finest woven straw objects known to the world are still being made. The process of gathering and preparing materials, and their transformation into functional objects, can be both utilitarian and spiritual.'

What is important is that in Australia there is strong government support for craftspeople and visual artists to enable them to work as professionals. The main funding body is the Australia Council which has several boards responsible for the various areas in the arts, such as the Aboriginal and Torres Strait Islander Arts Board and the Visual Arts and Crafts Board. Each state also has a Department for the Arts which makes money available to craftspeople and their professional organizations.

22

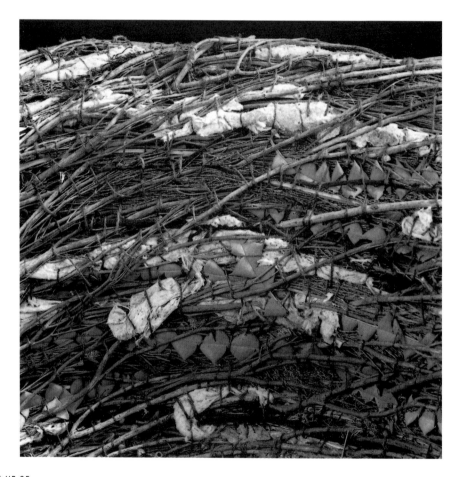

CLOSE-UP OF

WICKER BASKET.

Nalda Searles, like many Western Australian craftspeople, is a member of the Crafts Council of Western Australia, an organization subsidized by the Federal Government, whose activities and projects are aimed at promoting professional development for craftspeople, providing information for the communities and opening new markets, besides providing access to low-cost workshops for craftspeople. And above all, the Crafts Council staff are continually on the lookout for opportunities for their members to be involved in national and international craft events, often through their affiliation with Crafts Australia and the World Crafts Council.

As mentioned earlier, although Nalda's first introduction to textiles was through macramé, she has taught herself the techniques that she now uses to such great effect. For her, it is important that the method she has developed for creation with unusual materials be understood so that others may have the opportunity to learn the craft.

The most elementary technique in basket-making is the coiling method, whereby a long coil of fibre is circled around and then either wrapped or stitched into place to form the sides of the basket. Nalda discovered this method herself by using pieces of cloth and bits of string. Then she looked at the landscape and at the materials which she could find there. There were no palms available to make the long, strong lengths of fibre to form the basic framework in basketry. Instead, the materials were thin, brittle grasses, barks and twigs.

These were all very dry, so she had to find a way of making them hold together so that she could actually use them. Nalda began by bundling the grasses and twigs together and then splayed the bundles out before stitching them all together – each bundle becoming part of the surface of the basket.

She always looks for materials that will give texture, aroma, colour and strength. The materials are used straight from the bush without any preparation which means the art of the preparation is in the collecting, as she says, rather than in any modification of the materials such as boiling or dyeing.

Another technique that she has developed to consolidate her baskets and keep them in shape is to form ribs around the outside of the basket. She does this by incorporating twigs on the inside of the basket and then bringing them up into the coils so that they appear to be within the framework of the basket rather than around it. All these elements are held in place with linen thread stitched into place with a needle. The finished effect is a basket that is quite unique in that it does not have the usual regular woven surface but where we can clearly distinguish fragments of grass, twigs, flowers, and even bird-feathers and stones and the distinct aroma of the bush.

Nalda exhibits these baskets three or four times a year and they sell for between $A200 and $A500. One of her great satisfactions is derived from organizing exhibitions such as, among the latest, 'High Fibre Diet' and 'Street Art Children's Art' in 1994.

All these various aspects of her professional career show how active a person she is. She is very happy with her lifestyle and says of her chosen profession: 'Basketry has survived for a very long time and the demands on it are greater now than ever before in its history. For creators like ourselves, the art of innovation and creativity will enable this remarkable, tenacious art form to remain intact and relevant throughout future change.'

Today, Nalda Searles lives modestly in the hills of Kalamunda to the east of Perth, on the ground floor of a house surrounded by a large garden, where the bush is not far away.

Embera women: creative basket-makers of the Andes

by Lyda del Carmen Díaz López

Bogotá

The Emberas who, together with the Waunanas, make up the two major indigenous peoples in the southern part of the Pacific seaboard of Colombia, live in a region rich in natural resources. The communities living on the Sajia, Sanquianga, Naya and Cajambe rivers and their affluents are the Eperaras-Siapidaras, who call themselves 'Eperas' in accordance with the phonology of their dialect. Traditionally, these populations have always represented their vision of the world through various practices of an aesthetic nature. Whether it be the oral tradition, music, facial or body painting, or basketry, pottery, woodwork, weaving, ritual objects or the carving of canoes, all these practices combine to express and project their vision of human beings as individuals in ceremonial and daily activities in which nature and aesthetics combine. The life of these communities is based on subsistence agriculture and the cultivation of certain plant species such as the raffia palm used in handicrafts and the gathering of fruit and the selection of medicinal plants, while they supplement their diet with game hunted in the forest and fish from the rivers.

This was the context in which an association of craftswomen was set up, bringing together part of the population of the three indigenous territories of the Embera-

Eperara-Siapidara community. Five years ago, the Eperara women created two organizations composed of eighty craftswomen from some 900 families established in the districts of Nariño, Cauca and the Caucasia Valley.

The status of women in these areas and their involvement in all aspects of family life mean that they constitute the core or focal point of those communities, inasmuch as their activities contribute to both the development of the country and the safeguarding of its traditions and culture.

From their early teens, women in these communities take on the role of partners whose main tasks are procreation, working in the fields, looking after their families and making a contribution to community life as well as to traditional activities such as arts and crafts.

For Epera women, arts and crafts are a daily activity they have practised ever since they were children at their mother's side. They are also a determining factor in preserving the identity of the Embera populations and, today, have become one of the means whereby the community can establish links with the outside world while acquiring purchasing power according to the rules of the market economy.

Arts and crafts normally operate on two levels: one that is ritual, for the benefit of the

AN EPERA WOMAN
STARTS TO
WEAVE A BASKET.

community itself, and one focused on trade. It is the latter that enables such communities to establish links with the market economy which provides them with additional income for their subsistence and medical needs.

These women's educational level is poor, however, if not virtually nonexistent, marginalized as they are through early marriage. Most are illiterate as access to education is a very recent phenomenon and has scarcely gone beyond primary level. It is quite exceptional for any Embera woman to gain access to secondary or higher education.

They communicate with each in their native tongue and can rarely hope to establish relationships outside their own world. Their only opportunity for participation in community life is based on the distinction between female and male roles, with the male continuing to be the symbol of strength.

Basketry ranks as the main craft activity open to them. Eperara women produce objects of practical use in the life of the community: sleeping mats, baskets for carrying food, pokers for stirring kitchen fires and smaller baskets for storing personal effects. They also make toys for their children, imitating the form of familiar animals. Plant extracts are drawn from the various traditional crops, such as certain tinctorial plants, in the forest, as well as the *tetera* palm which provides most of the raw material used for the domestic market and is cultivated by women close to their dwellings in suitably damp hollows. Conversely, the *chocolatillo* is to be found at some distance from the villages and harvesting is linked to the phases of the moon. In both cases, it is the stem of these plants that is used for basketry.

The production process therefore begins with the cultivation of the plant and goes on to include the preparation of the fibres right

up to the actual fashioning of the object, its use and sale.

As regards the *tetera*, various tasks are involved which include preparing the soil, sowing, pruning, draining, weeding, cutting the stems, which are the usable part, scraping them and drying them. Then they are moistened and can be detached from the central core to form strips of 1–8 cm which are then left in the sun again to bleach. These strips are then washed, dried and cut into lengths according to the thickness required for weaving. If the finished article is to be coloured, then dyeing is required, either with vegetable dyes such as *achiote* or *mapushi*, dark types of mud or mineral dyes sold locally. As regards *chocolatillo*, the process involves gathering and carrying, followed by plant coloration or oxidation, by burying the fibres in muddy soil.

According to María de los Angeles González, an industrial designer, the technique usually used for this type of basketry is diagonal weaving, whereby the components are interwoven according to patterns of 1×1, 2×1, and $1 \times 2 \times 3 \times 4 \times 5$, thereby providing varied textures with motifs and symbols appearing on the objects. The basic principle is that of geometrical abstraction and the mathematical design of each effect means it can be repeated at regular intervals on the object. Diagonal weaving also gives considerable strength and means that the final product is of a high standard.

In this work, the craftswoman is responsible for the whole of the production process right up to the finished item; there is no male intervention at any time, except that of young boys helping their mothers with the crops. In the past, however, whenever surpluses were produced or certain quantities were reserved for the market, women no

PREPARING
THE WICKER
FOR WEAVING.

longer controlled the fixing of prices and marketing, which were then taken over by men.

The 'Productivo' project for the native craftswomen of Rio Sajia, set up five years ago by the traditional authorities to help craftswomen in their individual and family work, is backed by a convention between the Cauca Regional Autonomous Corporation and the European Community and also enjoys technical and commercial assistance from Artesanías de Colombia.

A preliminary survey brought to light those situations where women played a fundamental role in maintaining cultural identity and in child-rearing and were dissatisfied with the lack of co-operation and recognition on the part of men towards them – particularly with those who went off to the towns to sell their products, remained away from home and community for several days and never gave any account of the sales or the proceeds on their return. There was also evidence of the fear men felt on realizing women's desire to study and play a more decisive role in meetings and, more particularly, in community projects. This situation bred discontent and mistrust and often led to women being even more confined to the home.

When this was discussed between them, the men finally agreed to share responsibility for jointly defining the basis of the Craft Production Project, the main aim of which had always been 'to promote the participation of indigenous couples (men and women in partnership) in the administering, promotion and marketing of the craft project'.

One of the major issues was the enhancement of women's role in community life as custodians of culture.

The need was recognized by all to establish strong links between women and

school life and a better balance in strategies for literacy, exchange, participation in meetings with voting rights in regard to decision-making, as well as training, for both men and women, in accountancy and management which would enable them to acquire the basic skills for running their own projects.

The need was also recognized for women to learn to determine prices for their products and to enhance their craftwork by mastering such techniques as dyeing with industrial aniline and by reviving traditional know-how in the use of plants and mineral dyes while learning to make use of imported dyes. Women could use some of the income they derived from handicrafts to improve their homes, buy clothing and breed poultry.

Organizing craft groups or committees in each village, along traditional lines, would lay the foundations for a larger organization, the Rio Sajia Craftswomen's Association, the role of which would be to co-ordinate and develop local initiatives and act as a mediator between the groups and outside organizations, while facilitating the promotion and marketing of craft goods.

Improving products aimed at the national market was achieved by establishing direct links between the craftswomen and designers. Solutions were found, for example, to the technical problem of the brilliance of local indigo which the dyer could not guarantee to maintain between the workshop and the point of sale. Fixation of the colour could be achieved thanks to simple methods that the craftswomen could learn and by making use of additives to be found in their immediate environment. This collaboration between craftswomen and designers also provided various innovations with regard to finishing the edges, combining natural and artificial colours, transferring texture from one object to another and adopting forms for basketry

30

CRAFTWORK BY

EPERARA-SIAPIDARA

WOMEN.

that are usually confined to carpentry.

The products resulting from this experiment within the 'Incontro' project, funded by Artesanías de Colombia in various communities of the country, are now on display in galleries and museums in France, Germany, Italy, Spain and other European countries, after having been presented by the craftswomen themselves when they were invited to the Chilean Handicrafts Fair organized by the Catholic University and at the 1994 Colombia Creativa Exhibition of Handicrafts held at Santafé de Bogotá under the aegis of Artesanías de Colombia.

Participation in such events of a regional nature was experienced by craftswomen as a form of initiation in practices of the outside world and in the creation of links of solidarity between themselves and their partners through the opportunity of travelling together as men and women.

These women's future lies along this path.

They wish to pursue the Project for the Organization and Training of Indigenous Craftswomen along social lines and would like it to be part of an overall ethnological and educational plan. As a specific group, they contemplate, in a second phase, strengthening their local associations, planning marketing and entry into the production process, thereby reducing travelling costs and the need for their presence at points of sale. Mail-order catalogues would also provide them with access to the international networks of traditional arts and crafts.

In this way, Gabriella, Adelfa, Agustina and their companions, Embera craftswomen of Colombia, seek to assert their decision-making power in community and family life and, more particularly, develop their cultural, social and economic role for the benefit of their families and community and for their own fulfilment as women.

Ramrati: creator of fine terracotta

by Shalini Saran

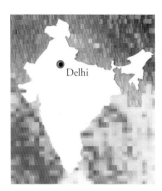

Delhi

It seems appropriate that a woman whose keen intelligence and insight grew from a close bonding with nature should express herself through the medium of clay.

Ramrati is now about 35 years old. She has six daughters – the eldest is 14 years old and the youngest 10 months. Her husband, Harkishan, is a fine man, a potter who has been nationally recognized as a master-craftsman.

After many years of struggling they have built themselves a small house in Uttam Nagar, a potters' colony on the outskirts of Delhi.

I first saw Ramrati's pots in her husband's workshop very near their house. Harkishan works on his motorized wheel in a cool, thatched shed, part of which serves as a store. There, in the midst of hundreds of pots of all shapes and sizes, Ramrati's work stood out for its exquisite colouring. A helper carried them out, and in the full light of day I realized I was looking at the work of an exceptionally gifted potter.

I have since spent long hours with Ramrati, seeing her at home, at work and interacting with buyers, and have found her spirit to be as exceptional as her talent.

Ramrati was born in a small village near Panipat, in the state of Haryana. She belongs to one of a few families of potters who met

their needs supplying earthenware to the village. They were landless and poor. Water was drawn from wells, the village had no electricity and it was linked to a bus service only when Ramrati was about 12. Two sisters having died in their infancy, she grew up with her brother, cherished by parents who were content with their lot.

'I was never forced to do anything', said Ramrati. 'If you put pressure on a child, there is no childhood. Mine was marked by freedom. I was happy and robust. At the age of 5 I was admitted to school, but on the first day I saw a child being beaten and decided never to go there again'. Ramrati loved most of all to care for the two buffaloes the family owned, and to roam the cultivated fields with those girlfriends of hers who owned land. 'Sometimes', she said, 'I helped my father prepare clay, or I painted designs on pots – the usual tasks performed by women in potters' families. But my father never liked me to work. He said that, once I was married, I would have to work anyway'.

Ramrati had no dreams or ambitions. 'I was so happy where I was, doing what I was doing, that I didn't even like to leave the village'.

The village had a largely Muslim population, though her family is Hindu. Festivals were social rather than religious

RAMRATI THE POTTER

WORKS CAREFULLY

TO ACHIEVE SUBTLE VARIATIONS

AND A FINE FINISH.

occasions. Ramrati has no recollections of any folk plays, or readings from the religious epics, the Ramayana and Mahabharata. No rituals specific to the caste of potters were observed, either.

The potter is known as *kumhar*, a word derived from *kumbhakaar* – *kumbh* meaning pitcher, and *akaar* form – that is, he who gives form to the pitcher. A potter is also known as *prajapati*, the creator of forms, after another name for Lord Brahma who, as Prajapati, made man out of clay. In place of religious conditioning, Ramrati developed a deep sense of being and an awareness of nature's bounty.

When Ramrati was 17, her father arranged for her marriage to Harkishan, who also belonged to a family of potters in a nearby village. 'His family was even poorer than ours, but my father was firm about his choice', she said. Marriage introduced Ramrati into a strange world of constraint, purdah (the practice of covering one's face with a veil before menfolk) and a taunting mother-in-law who would ask, 'All the daughters-in-law in this village are beaten by their husbands, why aren't you?' Ramrati spent most of the first three years of her marriage away from her husband, in her parental home. In the fourth year the couple moved to Delhi and it was only then that a relationship developed and grew into a wonderful understanding. The respect and love they have for each other is obvious even to a stranger.

Ramrati and her husband lived in a thatched hut on the very spot where their house now stands. 'At the time', said Ramrati, 'there were just about twenty families here. Most of the land, now built on, was cultivated. Harkishan's uncle gave us 250 rupees a month to assist him in making pots. It was difficult: two square meals a day were not assured. But we worked very hard, for I do believe that if you work you can feed yourself'.

Ramrati managed her home and her first-born and performed the traditional role of potter's wife. Some years went by before Harkishan received his first big break – he was selected to create special planters for a woman entrepreneur of the city. Ably assisted by Ramrati, he has worked hard, done well and been honoured, and on entering the colony one is directed to his workshop before one can even ask the way.

Their house is in the heart of the colony. It is rather untidy within, and very sparsely furnished. There is, however, a television and a telephone. The ground floor consists of three rooms, a kitchen and a courtyard with a kiln. The first floor has one room and a large terrace which affords a lively view of the colony. All around, in every home, one can see kilns, women at work preparing clay, and stacks of flowerpots and pitchers. This terrace is where Ramrati makes her pots, for ever since her eldest daughter reached puberty, she tries to spend what time she can at home.

I spent an afternoon watching her make a pot. When I arrived, the scene on the terrace could not have been more domestic. Ramrati, her six daughters and her widowed mother-in-law were all enjoying the winter sun. The baby was snug at Ramrati's breast, while the older girls, just back from school, were telling her about the events of the day even as they teased each other. I wondered how Ramrati could work here, but when she started she was poised and fully attentive.

Ramrati had kept two half-made pots to complete before me. From a lump of clay which had been prepared two days before, she rolled a coil about two and a half feet long and one and a half inches in diameter. She held one end of the coil up with her left hand. With her right hand she started fixing the other end of the coil along the rim of the pot, breaking off the coil when she reached the starting point. To strengthen this newly affixed layer she dipped her hand in water and pressed and smoothed the joint along the inner and outer surfaces of the pot. And so she progressed, using shorter lengths of coil till the pot, full and rounded at its centre, tapered to a small neck.

Only when the pot was complete did she step back to check its proportion and balance. Both were perfect. While the first pot was hardening in the sun, she completed the second. We had tea, the children continued to play, the older ones keeping the baby from crawling to her mother while one daughter, Sapna, sat behind Ramrati making little toys from clay.

Ramrati then turned to the first pot, and with a scraper she removed any roughness from its surface. She asked Poonam, the eldest girl, to prepare some colours. Poonam brought hard lumps of white hill clay and red clay, and pounded these separately into smooth powders, which Ramrati kneaded with water. Then, using a sharp instrument, Ramrati made shallow incisions on the surface of the pot with random strokes. Into these depressions she applied slips of red and white clay – again at random and with the same flexibility with which a painter applies colour. Then, using the scraper again, she smoothened the entire surface of the pot. As she did this, the colour blended subtly with the surface, and fluid patterns emerged accidentally. After both pots had been similarly treated, she waited a while, then polished their surfaces with a small, smooth oval piece of marble till the pots glowed. They were now ready for drying, which would take a few days. Firing would be done when a batch of eight to ten were ready.

When I asked Ramrati how long it had taken her to perfect this technique, she smiled and said, 'Can a human being ever create

anything perfect?'

Ramrati's growth from a traditional potter's wife to an individual artist as well, has been nurtured by a combination of circumstances and linked with her husband's career, but the moving forces have been her own creative mind and an indomitable spirit which has given her the courage to cross traditional boundaries – not an easy accomplishment for a woman of her social background.

About twelve years ago, Harkishan's first big assignment kept him away from home during the week, leaving Ramrati with spare time. 'It was then that I thought, why not try and make something with my hands, so I did, and the first thing I made', she said, laughing, 'was an aeroplane. Then I made a horse, then an elephant with a small pot on its back – all with my hands! I left them to dry in the sun. When my husband saw them he said, "If you want to be creative, make something beautiful. These should be broken!" You know, they were so coarse and so thick, I couldn't even break them. Ultimately I had to soak them in water and they dissolved.

'So my work began, with the shaping of small lamps, animal forms and so on. My husband made me break anything that was not reasonably okay. It used to hurt me, but it made me persevere. Truly, I have received nothing but encouragement from him'.

Once in a while Ramrati would accompany her husband on his assignment and help him decorate pots, making traditional designs with earth colours using a coarse brush. For a village woman who only spoke her dialect, the interaction with sophisticated urbanites was a totally new experience. 'I felt strange', she said, 'but I was not intimidated. It was there, too, that Gurucharan Singh, the famous potter, saw our work and encouraged us a great deal'.

Around this time Ramrati was given a large consignment of images of Lakshmi and Ganesh (deities worshipped at the festival of Diwali) to decorate. She earned 4,000 rupees for the job and was thrilled.

Ramrati did attempt to throw pots on the wheel, but it is traditionally believed by potters that the act of turning the wheel is harmful to the uterus. The motorized wheel has not made the logical difference it should have done, and it is most likely that the belief was yet another way to subordinate the position of women. 'Instead, I experimented with the coil method which women traditionally use to make earthen kitchen stoves. It took me some years to master this. In my earlier attempts, the coils would separate after firing. But I have since been able to make a variety of pots'.

One day, Harkishan took her to Pragati Maidan (Delhi's largest exhibition grounds) for a pottery exhibition. She said, 'It was then that I realized that my work was as good as, and in some cases better than, what I saw. It gave me confidence and I kept working. I got a part-time job at the Sriram School, teaching children to handle clay. I did it for a while and enjoyed it'.

Ramrati accompanied her husband to various crafts bazaars held in Delhi and other major cities and was soon handling stalls independently. Work increased at home, too. More children were born, and by now her husband could rely on her expertise to prepare the clay and complete the process once he had thrown a pot.

Till about four years ago, Ramrati's own work, though it had attained considerable refinement, was still fairly conventional terracotta. She had mastered the coil method to create pots of various shapes and sizes. But ornamentation comprised either relief work, engraving or painted designs. She even tried the oxidization technique, now popular amongst Delhi's potters, whereby the terracotta is partially blackened.

'One day', said Ramrati, 'as I was preparing colours, I dropped a lump of red clay into a pan of water. Gradually, the colour started spreading. I was enchanted by the effect and wanted to create something similar on clay. At first I tried kneading colours into the clay before shaping the pot, but it didn't please me. Slowly, by trial and error – and accident – I evolved the method I demonstrated'.

These recent works have won her considerable acclaim. In 1993 she received a state award for excellence. 'My husband had insisted that for this competition I send an individual entry'. Her work was also sent to the Festival of India in China in 1993–94. Ramrati is being recognized as an artist in her own right, and her pots have created a stir amongst connoisseurs.

It is true that her husband has supported her explorations. But it must also be remembered that Ramrati's search for self-expression has progressed alongside the demands of being a housewife, a mother to six children and fulfilling social responsibilities towards the extended family. Women of greater means than hers are known to have succumbed to such pressures.

Ramrati's work is rooted in traditional know-how, in the technique by which terracotta has been made in villages all over India for centuries. Today there are an estimated one million potters in India and they continue to be an essential part of the village community, supplying water vessels, grain storage containers and tiles for roofs.

The clay which they use is dug from river alluvium, natural ponds or clay pockets from hillsides. It is beaten into powder, sieved and then mixed with water and made into lumps

*RAMRATI WORKS
ON HER TERRACE WITH HER
DAUGHTERS WHO ARE
ALREADY WORKING IN CLAY.*

40

RAMRATI'S POTTERY:

REFINED AND

BEAUTIFUL SHAPES.

which are well-kneaded and stored for two days. This clay has a high content of silica, calcium, magnesium and especially iron, so that on burning the clay turns red. It is highly plastic and burns at a lower temperature than white clay.

Ramrati uses the same clay and prepares it in the same way as was done a century ago.

However, the method she employs for shaping her pots is a departure. The coil method was probably in use before the invention of the wheel, though there are tribes in Africa which still make large pots in this way.

Ramrati has evolved her decorating technique on her own, the finished effect of which resembles agate. It is not at all part of the Indian tradition, while it is commonly practised in Korea and Japan.

The technique is called the inlay process. It is interesting to note Ramrati's ability to appreciate and explore abstract forms that result from this process, as these are far removed from traditional Indian decorative motifs.

After firing their pots for many years in a traditional potter's kiln, an open, round updraught furnace heated with wood and sawdust and covered with broken bits of terracotta, Ramrati and her husband had a ceramic fibre dome made for them, which is placed on the kiln to conserve heat. The kiln can burn at a low temperature for about six hours.

Imperceptibly, the newly created products bear less resemblance to the traditional pitchers and grain storage containers. Their use is decorative and for an urban clientele.

Ramrati's work is imbued with the artist's delight in discovering the possibilities of a medium. When the process itself is an instrument of learning, it leads to a steady evolution. Now she has mastered every step of the process, she is much more attentive to what she can make.

An important consequence of Ramrati's work is that it has also added a whole new dimension to her marriage wherein her husband respects her as an equal.

On my advice, she visited the library at the Crafts Museum and looked at pictures of pottery from all over the world. She responded favourably and expressed delight at seeing samples of 5,000-year-old pottery at the National Museum.

Ramrati has no great urge to be literate, though she wishes she could write her accounts at bazaars. 'My daughters have tried to teach me. Believe me, they are worse than schoolmarms! I can write my name in the sand, but give me a pen and my fingers won't move!' She does, however, realize the advantage of literacy and is educating all her children.

Ramrati's major difficulty is that of most working women – the juggling of her time and energy between household reponsibilities and her profession. Even her professional time is divided, for her husband needs her expertise to assist in the completion of work orders, which are the major source of their income. And with eleven mouths to feed (in addition to the family of eight, her mother-in-law, brother-in-law and nephew live in), money is always welcome.

For the time being, Ramrati would like her recent work – so utterly different from that of other craftspersons – to be kept for an exhibition. It also means that for a while her work will bring no income. So it often happens that the time she devotes to her own work is erratic. Organizing a pottery exhibition will not be easy for her without guidance, since galleries prefer to exhibit paintings.

Her recent participation in the Annual

SKILFUL AND CREATIVE HANDS
WORKING THE CLAY TO
BRING OUT ITS QUALITIES.

Studio Potters Exhibition was a major acknowledgement of her talent. Ramrati is pleased, but not distracted by the recognition she has won, for she is at heart a very contented person. Harkishan teases her about her success. 'I think I'm the one', he says, 'who will soon be her assistant'.

Ramrati prefers to work in the second half of the day, when the children have gone to school and the household chores are done. If need be, she assists Harkishan late into the evening and sometimes makes her own pots at night.

Between October and March there are numerous crafts bazaars, and Ramrati is often away for the whole day. At such times, the housework is left to the eldest daughter. Guests, marriages and festivals create their own demands. Worship, however, is not a part of Ramrati's daily life. She says, 'If a hungry man comes to my door I will feed him, and to one who is lost I will show the way. If he needs money I will help him, but he must work for it and repay me when he can. This is what I believe . . .'.

Her hospitality is evident at home and at Harkishan's workshop where visitors and buyers come. The atmosphere is relaxed. They pay a rent of 500 rupees a month for about 400 sq. yds. of land, adequate space to accommodate large work orders. In the afternoons, the children play while helping their parents.

I have seen Ramrati dealing with buyers. She is a shrewd businesswoman, more exacting than her husband, and is nobody's fool. She had even brought a daughter of hers to a crafts bazaar I visited and was letting her handle the clients. 'How else will she learn to raise her voice?' asked Ramrati. Though the market is becoming increasingly competitive, these bazaars are regular outlets for their work. They also serve as points of contact between craftspeople, bulk buyers and exporters.

The couple's position within the country's economic framework is positive at many levels. Since independence, traditional craftspeople have once again been given importance and 'handmade' items are valued. In a growing urban consumer society, ethnic chic is 'in'.

Labour is still cheap in India, and exporters are quick to realize the benefits of applying contemporary design to traditional skills. All these factors contribute to the growing prosperity of semi-urban and urban craftspersons like Harkishan and Ramrati.

Ramrati does not look too far into the future. Her plan is to continue working, experimenting with new colours and shapes, trying glazes, for example, which no one here has attempted yet. Ramrati would like to demonstrate her skills at the Crafts Museum in Delhi and, given the chance, to travel abroad.

Her husband was sent to Japan and Spain and she was impressed to hear from him that neither country has a caste system, and that the gap between rich and poor there is insignificant.

As a woman Ramrati is a curious mix of traditionalist and rebel. She is determined to give her daughters the best possible education she can afford. 'Regardless of what their father thinks, I have one desire for my daughters – that they have the freedom to choose what they want to do'.

I asked her if she knew that women were fighting for their rights. 'Yes', she said, 'I have heard that, and I think they should. But I'll tell you one thing, women allow themselves to be suppressed. And if you let a man suppress you, he will sit upon you like a lion'.

For herself, there are no drawbacks in being a woman. She confessed to me at our last meeting that she was pregnant again. In the hope of having a son, her husband does not agree to a vasectomy.

'Besides', says Ramrati, 'if he has a vasectomy he will lose the strength to make large pots' (the lack of strength and virility as a result of vasectomy are prevalent misconceptions).

'My body is strong, and there is enough to eat in the house. Tell me, why should I not have children?'

Her family, her home and her work are Ramrati's major priorities. She has neither the temperament nor the time to be an activist of any kind. Her husband has political alignments, but Ramrati does not trust politicians.

The women in the colony respect her. She says that if any one of them came to her to learn how to make pots, she would help. 'But they are so burdened with work', she says. 'These women lack the spirit, and one's spirit is most important, it makes everything possible . . .'.

Ramrati is embarking on a new journey and exploring further frontiers.

I have faith that her creative mind and her determined spirit will, as in the past, be her true guides, and I wish her well.

Mel Bradley: hand-painted silk

by Mairead McAnallen

Dublin

London 1993, and the spring/summer fashion season is at its height. As the fashion designer John Rocha emerges on to the cat-walk, the audience gives a standing ovation to the show that will shortly win him the Designer of the Year Award. The model at his side wears a sheath of silk; dramatically painted with one enormous red poppy. Few, if any, amongst this audience know the name of the Irish craftswoman who painted it.

In the twelve years since she began to make her reputation with her hand-painted scarves, Mel Bradley has become Ireland's most successful craftswoman in the field of textiles. Her sometimes flamboyant, sometimes subtly coloured scarves are sold in shops throughout the country, and in the five years since 1990 her silks have become an important part of the collections of two of the country's most distinguished fashion designers. Through them, her work is seen on the cat-walks of London and Paris and is exported to France, Hong Kong, Italy, Saudi Arabia and the United Kingdom.

She is a woman of quiet determination with a clear vision of what she wants from the world and, on a superficial reading, it looks as if her successful career has been very carefully charted.

In 1979, Mel entered the College of Marketing and Design in Ireland's capital city,

Dublin, moving the following year to the National College of Art and Design. Wishing to bring her interests in design, colour and fashion together, she enrolled in the Department of Fashion and Textiles, specializing in printed textiles. There she learned to draw and gained the knowledge of cutting and pattern-making that support her work with fashion designers now.

She graduated in 1981 and six months later was accepted at the Kilworth Craft Workshops, a project of the Crafts Council of Ireland that trains young craftspeople in the business skills necessary to set up their own studios. At the end of her year at Kilworth, she had a product – printed silk scarves – and a business plan to present to banks and the state agencies that could provide setting-up grants. She had attended her first trade fair and had been well received by the people who could retail her scarves.

After a disappointing attempt at working in partnership, she set up alone in Dublin in 1983, in the supportive environment of the Tower, a centre dedicated to the crafts, subsidized by the Industrial Development Authority (IDA). Her father's guarantee was used to secure the bank loans necessary to provide for her equipment. A print-table was made, and as the first materials were brought, Mel started to paint on fabric and found that

MEL BRADLEY AT WORK:

TREE PAINTING ON SILK

FOR THE JOHN ROCHA 1994

AUTUMN/WINTER COLLECTION.

she liked it. When the silk screens she had ordered arrived, they were used as stretchers for the silk she painted.

For the first four years, Mel worked alone. Since that time, she has always had at least one assistant, one of whom has her own silk-painting business now. Today she has two full-time assistants, and one part-time.

From the beginning, she had simply made scarves and then gone out and sold them, either at the annual Crafts Trade Fair or to large organizations who used them as corporate gifts, and she sometimes made dresses for individual clients, friends and friends of friends.

Then came a definite turning-point in the form of collaboration with the fashion designer, Louise Kennedy. 'Our first project did not work at all – the silks shrank! But in 1990, we made our first complete season's designs, basically a scarf to complement a woollen fabric with a diamond design. It was immediately popular and led to a regular order for sixty or seventy new wraps each season.' In 1995's first fashion season, Mel has supplied Louise Kennedy with 120 full-size wraps which sell in the fashion stores at about $380.

As a result of this success she met John Rocha, a Japanese designer living and working in Dublin, who wanted to develop unique fabric designs of his own, and their collaboration has been successful to the point where Mel Bradley's silks were a major part of his 1993 London show. They were first presented on the Paris cat-walks in autumn 1994. The poppy dress that made Rocha famous in 1993, now part of the collection of the Leeds Museum in England, originated in a scarf that Mel designed for him.

Mel Bradley was blessed at birth with the talents of both her mother's and father's lineages. The second of five children, she was born in Dublin in 1958. Her father was self-employed as a jewellery wholesaler throughout his working life. 'In fact, the whole family was self-employed; we were all down in the office on Saturday morning, filling out forms and packing jewellery in boxes to send out on order. I grew up knowing that you work for what you get. You know, anything can go wrong when you are self-employed. You can get sick, for example, and this is important when you work on your own as Dad did.'

They moved to the town of Wicklow, thirty-two-miles south of Dublin, when Mel was 9. 'I loved Wicklow and made very good friends there while I was at school. Of course, it was a small country town, and we had the freedom to cycle to the beach, go mountaineering and blackberry-picking in country lanes – always in gangs – my own age group was much more important then than my parents!'

The dramatic hills, valleys, coastline and luxuriant forests of the Wicklow countryside provide one of Europe's most beautiful landscapes, and the young Mel, with her innate sense of visual awareness, must have absorbed some of the sense of nature's pattern and colour that inspires her adult work. She remembers these years as idyllic, and was unhappy when the family moved again when she was 17, this time to Greystones. On the eastern seaboard, like Wicklow and Dublin, Greystones was, however, within commuting distance of the capital and the art colleges.

The greatest influence came from her maternal grandmother who had been a costumier for the theatre and was a wonderful dressmaker. Her house was full of sewing, costumes, cloth and bags of cloth. 'You would be afraid to sit down in case you sat on a sewing needle! She met my grandfather when she was 16 years old. He owned a firm of theatrical costumiers, and all my aunts worked in the business too. I sometimes worked with

48

them as wardrobe mistress in the Olympia Theatre in Dublin and, of course, we always made things at home, my grandmother, mother and I. We never drew; we just designed with fabric, although we were not conscious that we were designing. I did not know what that meant until I went to the College of Marketing and Design.'

Between the ages of 15 and 18, fascinated by a vivacious nun who taught her domestic science at school, Mel decided she wanted to be a teacher too. The desire lasted for a number of years until, influenced by an Austrian, an artist for whom Mel worked as an au-pair after leaving school, she turned down a place at teacher training college and opted for an art education instead.

As a student she met her husband, Donagh, in Greystones. He worked in a bank and 'he thought that what my friends and I made was rubbish! He is a very accurate draftsman and a good cartoonist.' They married in 1986 and have a son, Ciaran, who is 4 years old now. 'He refuses to draw at school and his teacher worries about disappointing me, but I do not want my son to be a performing flea! He likes to make things with clay and smash them up again, but he prefers lawnmowers and Batman.'

They lived and worked in Dublin until 1994, when Donagh was promoted in the bank and moved to manage his own branch in the town of Drogheda. Now they live in Laytown, little more than a village that straggles along the seafront, seven miles south of Drogheda and Mel commutes to Dublin, 30 miles away. Travelling takes up two or three hours of every day, depending on whether she drives or takes the train.

They were able to buy their house but, up to now, Mel has been too busy to furnish it according to her own taste. Finding the bathroom particularly depressing, she tore the wallpaper down about four months ago, but still has to find the time to decide on a new colour scheme and redecorate it. Only the kitchen-dining room, which extends into a marvellous conservatory and looks south over fields and distant hills, gives a clue to her own taste and personality. There are some colourful prints and batiks from the Caribbean, and a variety of thriving pot-plants stand out against fresh, white-painted walls, forming a pattern reminiscent of Mel's lush, painted silks.

'I'm not the ideal bank manager's wife. I am quite happy that Donagh and I have parallel lives, each of us doing our separate things and meeting up in the family, and socially as a couple.'

'I don't like going out with people I don't know, because my time is short.'

As the years go by, Mel finds that their work and their growing son provide them with a lot of interests, and the few friends suffice who understand and reciprocate the effort of keeping in contact.

There is something about the woman's calm energy and the ease with which she moves through life that is all of a piece with Mel Bradley's choice of craft. The ancient techniques of silk painting originated in China, like silk itself.

Silk paints are very different from those used on thicker fabrics like wool and cotton. They are, with some exceptions, translucent rather than opaque, and sink into the fibres rather than sit on the surface so that the silk retains its natural sheen, softness and flexibility.

The *serti* method of silk painting used by Mel Bradley requires the silk to be stretched taut across a frame to enable the outlines of the desired pattern to be drawn on with *gutta* – a dye-resistant gum (from the *gutta* tree) which acts like a wax, containing the dye within the outline. This means that different colours can be painted on side-by-side, separated by the *gutta* outlines.

Later the colour will be fixed by steaming, any excess dye will be washed out under running water, and the *gutta* can be removed by washing or dry cleaning. The colours are strong and vibrant, but they can be softened to pastel with dilution.

In fact, the years of reading and experience have allowed her to adapt considerably the basic *gutta* techniques she began with. Her use of the pipette, which gives a finer line, supplemented that of the *tjaunting*, a Far Eastern instrument used in batik, and Mel's skill with both tools shows in her free-flowing and, very often, voluptuous drawing – one of the studio's hallmarks. She also discovered that a complete length of fabric could be treated with *gutta* in much the same way as a painter treats a canvas. This gives the greater flexibility of being able to paint directly on to the silk, even to sponge colour on, and the paint will stay exactly where it is put. The technique also facilitates subtle colour changes across a length of silk, another characteristic of Mel Bradley designs.

Along with the depth of her mastery of the basic method, an instinctive control of pattern, the sweeping, fluid lines of her drawing and the breadth of palette she commands (dramatic reds, blacks, plum-purple and shocking pink for John Rocha, watered blues, subtlest greens and greys, and the full range of pastels for Louise Kennedy), and you have a craftswoman of great distinction.

In complete contrast with the rural backdrop of her domestic life and the reflective nature of her craft, the business – Mel Bradley Hand-Painted Silks – is conducted in the heart of working-class Dublin.

The Tower was built in the mid-eighteenth century as a sugar refinery and warehouse. It overlooks the basin of the Grand Canal – a Victorian highway of commerce leading into the dockland area of the River Liffey only a short distance away. Mel now occupies two studio spaces on the sixth floor. In the larger one, most of the floor area is occupied by free-standing work surfaces, giving the first clue to the quantity of work that passes through. The floor-level windows are spaced widely along two of the walls, making the use of artificial light necessary all day long.

Early in the morning, Mel's senior assistant, Katie, is found drawing the *gutta* outlines of a design on to a length of silk. Elsewhere Andrea is 'painting by numbers', brushing brightly coloured dyes into the spaces Katie has defined to bring the picture to life. Behind her, the tall, cylindrical steamer is at work, fixing the colour in some finished lengths.

Mel brushes *gutta* across a length of silk – in the afternoon it is to be given a new sponged design for Louise Kennedy. Three different orders are being worked on today.

Next door in the little studio where Mel originally set up her workshop, Lisa is at work, trimming and ironing scarves and wraps in preparation for finishing. The edges will be rolled and sewn by out-workers unless they are part of a very big order, in which case they may be sent to England to be rolled by machine. This room also serves as a display area where visitors can choose from a selection of scarves kept for direct sale.

These three young women take much of the responsibility for turning out the regular, repeat orders. Katie has worked here for two years and, apart from doing most of the drawing with *gutta*, she modifies patterns from Mel's first designs to suit scarves of different shapes and sizes, deals with clients when Mel

50

'MARDI GRAS',
AN ORIGINAL
GEORGETTE CRÊPE SHAWL
BY MEL BRADLEY.

52

'PARASOLS' , A
CRÊPE DE CHINE SCARF
BY MEL BRADLEY.

is away, and directs and supervises much of the main production.

Andrea, still learning the basic skills, paints to Katie's instructions, mixes dyes, stretches fabrics and takes care of steaming.

Lisa works a half-week, washing, ironing, packing, sorting and giving reliable help with quality control. She and Katie both help with selling to visitors who call at the Tower.

Mel Bradley is one of a minority of Irish craftspeople who take time to build up stock in addition to completing special orders. 'We have four months' stock to hand at any time,' she says, 'and putting the time of four people

into making this is a risk because we may not sell it. But, if it is not there, there is nothing to sell. I am still learning about the need for flexibility and the ability to adapt continuously if a business like this is to run well. The tasks that seem really important this morning may have moved far down the list of priorities by lunch time – it could happen that the batch of silk I started to work on turns out not to take the dye evenly, for example. Then I have to start again with a new batch and the order of work for the day will be completely upset.'

The work changes very quickly from day

to day, which can be very demanding. Clients inevitably confirm orders late, and then the days can be long.

'I often wonder why I bother to run this small business. There is no real financial incentive to employ people, there are so many barriers. It costs much more to employ someone than the pay they take home, and if my business closed down tomorrow, I am the only one who would be left with nothing. I would not be entitled to Social Welfare, maternity benefit or any of the benefits that would apply to my employees. I often think that our government doesn't really encourage the kind of self-employment that almost comes naturally to women, the kind of businesses where response can be quick and adapted to suit a particular demand – where collaboration and flexibility are necessary. Women are good at that – the skills demanded are similar to the ones we learn growing up, taking care of a household economy, bringing up children and looking after other people. I think governments could harness women's energies and experience much, much better.

'If my business were not small, it would not have been possible suddenly to produce two new designs very quickly for John Rocha and complete a batch of scarves for Louise Kennedy as I did this week. If we were bigger, this would seriously interrupt production. So the business will always remain small. But that means that the amount I can pay staff will always be limited. In the craft field, you are always aware that for your employees this cannot be considered as a career. Most employees move on to a different job or set up their own businesses.

'I have my own disposable income, and this is important to me. If I were not married, I would have to watch my pennies more carefully, but I could own a house and live reasonably well. I do not know if the income I

make is commensurate with the hours I work, and I could certainly earn just as much for myself, doing only special production for the fashion designers – but how long will this work last? How are fashion trends going to develop? So I do not run my business for any major economic reason. I do it because I love what I do.'

The work is composed roughly 50 per cent of her own original scarf designs for Irish shops and 50 per cent of work to fashion designers' specifications. 'They value my work, and that of all of the people who embroider and knit for them. They appreciate that we make a considerable contribution to their success.'

In reality, all of her work is addressed to the fashion world – a world which is tempered with common sense. 'Donagh and I were invited to the party after John's fashion show, but we left, bored, after an hour. I mean, what is there to say to one hundred famous people? You can't really have a conversation.'

Although marketing is not needed at present, fashions change and shops close down, and it is necessary to look to the future. The Irish national airline, Aer Lingus, has sold Mel's scarves through its in-flight duty-free shops for a number of years. Now they say they want higher profit margins in 1995 and Mel has been asked to reduce her prices. 'We will come to some solution this year, but I will not continually cut my prices. I am planning to sell abroad through the Irish Trade Board and I will create new designs and take them to the London shops.'

Other changes are planned for the future; Mel has been drawing a firmer line between her assistants' work and her own and looking for a second studio nearer to home for her use alone.

'Donagh and I considered converting the garage, but we agree that if work is not located away from home I will not be able to confine my working hours at all. As it is, all the paperwork is done at home in the evenings and at weekends, and at night I even sew while watching television. I'm getting to be like my grandmother – scarves littering the sofas and driving Donagh crazy! So I am trying to rent a new studio in Drogheda.

'The regular production will continue in Dublin, but I will not need to travel there every day. And that means I will be able to get home by five o'clock and have dinner at a reasonable hour, and spend more time with my son. Of course, I may not make scarves forever!' Her face lights up. 'The big plan is to get together with friends and make my own range of clothes.' Serious again: 'But I would want time to do it properly.'

Yes, although Mel Bradley's life gives the impression of having been well mapped out, in fact, things have developed simply – but according to a logic shaped by her self-assurance. Life seems to unfold for her because she has the self-assurance to choose lightly the things – relationships, responsibilities and involvements – that she needs, and to refuse to admit others. She is a woman free of conflicts.

'Designing is about listening to what other people want or need, this is the framework in which the designer creates – by solving problems. I always do my best to deliver what is wanted, when it is wanted. Nowadays I am better at telling clients when I am in trouble, and they usually understand; besides, I have never let my quality slip. In twelve years I have only once had a scarf returned to me because it went wrong.

'And last of all, do you know the saying, "Saturday's child works hard for a living"? Well, I was born on Saturday, I do work very, very hard.'

She smiles: 'Of course, I am also a subject of Cancer – a natural home-maker.' The interview ends in a peal of laughter.

M'athabo Victoria Nthako: clay-modeller

by Tsokolo 'Muso

Maseru

Where out of dust the Creator made man and woman, M'athabo Victoria Nthako makes images of animals, vegetation and scenes out of clay. M'athabo, whose name means 'Mother of Gladness', is the contemporary lady-artist of distinction in the 'Kingdom in the Sky', a fashionable name for Lesotho. M'athabo Nthako's hand-painted clay figurines have won her praise and an entry in the Lesotho Women Artists' Yearbook. Curio-hunters and indigenous art collectors who have spent moments exploring the small galleries in Teyateyaneng, Lesotho's arts and crafts market town, usually go past M'athabo's 'Bataung Pottery' that is situated by the side of the main Maseru road and adjacent to the St Agnes Anglican Church education mission.

The unobtrusive sign at the side of the road is the only pointer to M'athabo's remarkable pottery collection. One of the Kingdom's most gifted women artists is almost unsung. Born in 1952 at Kubere village in the Lekokoaneng peri-urban settlement, she is the youngest of three children and the only daughter. The Zizi splintered into groups of a family of pastoral farmers, of the Bafokeng clan of a branch renowned for their artistic creations of clay, wood and beads, who settled in the grassy mountain plateau of Lesotho long ago.

Apart from the artistic legacies flowing from her ancestors, M'athabo was actually taught the art of clay-modelling by her own mother, M'athabiso, who found life in the land of her husband boring and uneventful. So she started making clay pots that were much needed for storing beer, sour milk, and water, and dishes as well as other utensils used for food. She sold her products and educated her five children.

M'athabo herself was educated up to junior certificate level which enabled her to teach from 1974 to 1988 at the St Agnes Anglican Primary School. Since then, M'athabo has been self-employed. Like her mother, she was forced by circumstances to go back to clay-modelling, if only for sheer survival.

What is the role of art in the overall lifestyle of Africans in southern Africa? M'athabo has only a vague idea of the importance of art in the cultural development of her country. She participates in arts and crafts exhibitions that are held annually by the Lesotho arts and crafts trade fair. Started by some individual citizens of the United States Peace Corps Mission in Lesotho, the fair is the responsibility of the Lesotho Chambers of Commerce and Industry.

'M'athabo's figurines are part of a great cultural drive,' writes Derek Alberts, a

M'ATHABO VICTORIA NTHAKO
SHOWS SOME OF
HER CLAY FIGURINES.

journalist who visited Taung Pottery recently. 'Every work of art', writes Hampaté Ba, 'is like a silent word. Everything speaks, everything around us imparts a mysterious, enriching state of being.'

In her workshop-sanctuary, M'athabo makes clay images by a mysterious analogy, the initial act of creation, thus participating in the central mystery of life.

She has to be seen hard at work to be understood and appreciated properly.

She often draws inspiration from the Bible and many of her group figurines depict Old Testament scenes such as Eve tasting the forbidden fruit, Daniel in the lions' den and Abraham sacrificing his son.

From year to year, M'athabo's work has shown greater precision and refinement. She has successfully followed in the footsteps of Ts'itso Mohapi, the current Honorary Patron of the Lesotho Academy of Arts, who is noted for his figurine of two young Basotho men playing a game of *morabaraba* or draughts (a traditional game introduced in the nineteenth century by French missionaries).

Another influence in the artist's work is Samuel Makoanyane, a descendant of the founder of the Basotho nation and the first clay-modeller whose works have been widely publicized outside Africa and have attracted the attention of foreign art collectors. Thus the cultural context in which M'athabo works is conducive to preoccupations in artistic creativity.

M'athabo's change of career has not been easy: she abandoned teaching to pursue artistic fulfilment and has sought a simpler style. Her technique is quite simple: 'I sift the clay and knead it until it is smooth like butter', she says. 'After making a sculpture, I first dry it in the house for a while before firing it in the kiln.' The kiln in question is made of sods and smeared with mud. It is as old as humanity, for it has also been used by iron-smelters from time immemorial.

Today, M'athabo has to bring up her five children on her own. Her husband, Kefuoe, a farmer, part-time watch-repairer and evangelist preacher, was drowned recently in the river Tebetebeng at a baptism ceremony.

M'ATHABO FINDS
HER INSPIRATION IN
THE NATURAL WEALTH OF
THE PLATEAUX.

He used to help her in her pottery work by going to fetch the clay she needed.

She is now helped in her work by her eldest son, Thabo, aged 19. She also enjoys the encouragement and support of people who believe in her talent, such as the Harrisons, a British couple who recently visited her, Linda and Graham Taylor, who run the Kolonyama Pottery gallery, and Margaret Waller in Harare.

But here, in Lesotho, the market for arts and crafts is limited and tourism is only seasonal, so artists live from hand to mouth. The problem is to have access to outside markets. Yet M'athabo is a young, resourceful woman. 'I have never been to Natal and I want to show my work in Pietermaritzburg and in Durban! I admit that my clay figurines are fragile but they can be put in display cabinets like ancient Egyptian figurines or like some of our own ancient objects such as the *merifi* (pitchers), *mepotjoana* (cups) and *likotlol* (dishes) which have become collector's items.'

There is a good chance that M'athabo will be appointed professor of ceramics at the Lesotho Academy of Arts.

Tsokolo 'Muso: Did you teach art, among other subjects, when you were employed as a primary school teacher?

M'athabo Nthako: Yes, I did, but only now and then.

T. M.: Why only now and then?

M. N.: I was overloaded with work and had too many pupils.

T. M.: But isn't art as important as any other school subject?

M. N.: Art, like music, dance and drama, is generally regarded as something you do when you have nothing better to do.

T. M.: What do children do when it is time for an art lesson?

M. N.: When I was at school, we used to play or sing by ourselves.

T. M.: So you were never taught drawing, painting, wood or stone carving, nor how to read and write music, nor how to dance?

M. N.: That's all Dutch to me. When it was time for music, we sang traditional or children's lyrics. These are simple, repetitive tunes, nothing like the songs of Mohapeloa or Enoch Sontonga.

T. M.: With the gift of clay modelling in your blood and from the influence of your mother, who will you pass this legacy on to?

M. N.: To my own children.

T. M.: How about the children in your neighbourhood?

M. N.: The children are inspired by my son's clay animals. The kids would very much like to learn clay-modelling, but their parents say that I'm just play-acting. There were no art schools in Lesotho when I was young. Today art, dance and drama are taught at the Machabeng High School in Maseru which attracts a large number of children from foreign countries. Their parents are educated in one or more of these or are aware of the importance of art in life and in education. The Lesotho Academy of Arts is recruiting more and more people from South African schools of art.

T. M.: What role do you really think art should play in the life of your country?

M. N.: Art, to me, is a vital part of our way of life. It helps us to live life well and teaches us how to think, feel, look, eat, sleep and how to live. Living is an art.

T. M.: What is the economic importance of art?

M. N.: One of my teachers used to say that 'the material prosperity of a country relies

59

entirely on the skills of its inhabitants'. I believe that investment in art education can only enrich the Basotho and liberate Lesotho from mental, spiritual, moral, physical, economic and social poverty.

T. M.: Can you tell, M'athabo, what work you are doing now?

M. N.: Since my husband's untimely death, I am in mourning and, because of custom, have had to suspend my modelling activities for at least twelve months.

T. M.: But how are you going to afford your children's schooling if you don't sell your figurines?

M. N.: My husband's people, especially his brothers, will provide me with support till the time comes for me to resume my work.

T. M.: Does this mean you have completely abandoned your art and are doing nothing?

M. N.: Not totally. My son Thabo is taking over from me and has assembled ten of his school friends to show them how to make models of animals and persons. Tradition allows me to supervise his work.

T. M.: Do they manage to sell what they produce?

M. N.: Oh, yes. There is an open arts and crafts market in the centre of Maseru, the capital. Thabo takes turns with his friends in taking their images for sale, mainly to tourists, every Saturday morning. I must admit, however, that we barely manage to survive with the earnings from our Maseru market.

T. M.: And what are your future plans?

M. N.: For the future of my clay-modelling art, I first of all nurture a dream, and then I have to face reality.

T. M.: And what is your dream?

M. N.: I dream of a school of ceramics in my country, fully equipped with ovens and working tools and staffed by trained and experienced professional ceramists, teachers and administrators. The school would make maximum use of the wealth of clay deposits to be found in Lesotho and would include talented sculptors and clay-workers, regardless of their level of academic achievement. The ultimate goal of my dream school is to liberate every artist from slavery. When broken down, this concept means that each and every individual artist or designer, whatever is being created, must be self-employed if he or she is to lead a creative life.

T. M.: What do you mean by slavery?

M. N.: The co-operative movements tell us that many people's work is underpaid in order to enrich their employers. Now, being self-employed, I'm nobody's slave and labour disputes have no place in my economic scheme.

T. M.: Now, my last question relates to your assessment of your role as a model for other craftswomen in Lesotho.

M. N.: That is a billion dollar question! I am not a prophet nor a fortune-teller! My immediate answer would be that every artist who succeeds in overcoming countless obstacles is an inspiration to up-and-coming colleagues. Should I succeed in converting my dream into reality, any number of Basotho clay-modellers will rise to fame in the field of ceramics.

My son Thabo's work makes mine look amateurish. I am merely a switch that serves to light a darkened room.

Aminata Traoré: bringing the wealth of a tradition to light

by Fatoumata Agnès Diaroumeye

The 120 African artists meeting in Brazzaville (Congo) in July 1994, under the aegis of UNESCO, were addressed by a woman in the following terms: 'The crisis our countries are struggling with is, first and foremost, eminently cultural rather than political, economic and financial. Africa's debt has grown precisely because we no longer like what we produce and others are ready to sell us, whether we like it or not, both the essentials and the superfluous'.*

Aminata Traoré's life and work express her constant struggle against this situation which she believes to be intolerable. Guest-houses such as 'Djenné', 'San Toro' and the 'Amadou Hampaté Ba Centre' are various places in Bamako where she has proved that life could be otherwise. These places are undeniably the custodians of 'memory', a concept as well as a function to which Aminata attaches great importance. As she reminded African artists at Brazzaville: 'Unlike other social actors, you don't make do with a borrowed identity, you have a memory of your own and you are the memory of the continent. You have talent.

Africa needs men and women of talent to reinvent the present and the future. . . . Africa needs a new and exalting vision.'

At first glance, there was nothing in the academic background of Aminata Traoré – Amy to her friends – to suggest that she would commit herself in such a way to the artistic and cultural development of her country and of Africa at large.

Conversely, her childhood, family background and the social, political and economic development of her country provided a favourable environment for the blossoming of this awareness and combative spirit which are the hallmarks of her personality.

She has unceasingly struggled for and championed the cause of women, young people and an independent, democratic and sovereign Africa. Aminata divides her time between defending ideas and action in the field.

The ill-informed observer may be surprised by the scope and diversity of the activities in which Aminata is involved. There is, nevertheless, a guiding thread between her research, her participation in national, regional or international meetings and the action in which she is involved.

A relentless worker, constantly beavering away, Aminata is boisterous, generous and

---

* *Final Report of the Pan-African Colloquium in Brazzaville (Congo) on the Living and Working Conditions of Artists,* Paris, UNESCO, July 1994.

MODERN AND DYNAMIC AND
PROFOUNDLY AFRICAN,
AMINATA CLEVERLY COMBINES
TRADITIONAL TECHNIQUES AND
CONTEMPORARY CREATIVITY.

cheerful. While constantly up in arms against injustice, harassment and poverty, she also has a particular attachment to family relationships and friendship that endears her to all. This particular aspect of her personality, which accounts for the diversity of her friends' cultural origins, is rooted in the African culture, particularly that of Mali, which, nevertheless, is universal.

Aminata is one of those rare Africans who have managed to preserve and cultivate their cultural identity while exposing themselves to other cultures, namely those that represent a link between the various peoples of Africa, and between Africa and the rest of the world. She is one of those people who act as 'go-betweens', whereby the difference that exists with others is a serenely enriching experience.

Consequently, the work of artistic creativity and social transformation in which Aminata is involved in Bamako can be likened to both an insight into oneself and an outgoing approach to others.

All mediums and all forms of expression strike her as useful in rehabilitating Malians and Africans in general and in asserting their presence in the world. She endeavours to ensure that they can identify with her approach. For instance, she has been entrusted by the government authorities with decorating many ministerial offices and an increasing number of amateurs and shopkeepers have adopted the style and type of decoration that she is promoting.

As for foreigners, they see 'Djenné' and 'San Toro' as guest-houses where they can discover or rediscover what Malian and African arts and crafts have to offer at their best and most original, settings that enable them to appreciate the paintings of Abdoulaye Konaté, Ismael Diabaté, Ibrahima Koné and Kra Kadjo, for example, as well as superb pottery, weaving and fabrics in *bogolan.*

Clothes and jewellery feature quite prominently in Aminata's activities, as is immediately obvious when one meets this handsome woman who knows perfectly how to set them off to advantage.

She was the first woman to wear *fori,* the large Peul earrings, in circles where people were not accustomed to seeing traditional jewellery. She collects everything from bracelets to necklaces and ear-rings but soon parts with them by making generous presents of them to friends and acquaintances.

As a Malian woman, Aminata is profoundly attached to her country in spite of the success she has achieved abroad. Between 1975 and 1988, when based in Côte d'Ivoire, she often travelled between Abidjan where she was working and Bamako where her parents lived. Her house in Abidjan, in the Deux Plateaux district, was the first place where she expressed her love for art, handicrafts and decoration that she conveyed to all those around her. However, as her variety of interests expanded, her house in Côte d'Ivoire became all the more cramped whereas in Bamako, she had more space at her disposal.

This is how, between 1983 and 1987, she designed and built the 'Djenné' restaurant and exhibition rooms and, subsequently, the 'San Toro' in 1993. In addition to being a particular type of restaurant, the latter establishment has a gallery and a garden which serve as an excellent venue for all sorts of events.

In the following year, 1994, she created the Amadou Hampaté Ba Centre, named after the eminent Peul sage, defender of African traditions. Aminata would like to make of her centre something exemplary and thereby contribute to fostering greater interest in the development of Mali and Africa as a whole, in collaboration with other researchers, artists and intellectuals.

In the course of various interviews, we were able to listen to Aminata Traoré speak with satisfaction and enthusiasm of her origins, the childhood that left such a mark on her, her years of study, the path that led her towards arts and crafts, her research and her plans for the future. Let us now listen to what she has to say.

'I should say, first of all, that I have had two mothers. My first mother, Bintou Sidibé, brought me into the world in Bamako, one day in 1947.

'She was one of the most gifted dyers of her generation and had mastered the techniques of dyeing with indigo. I can still remember those enormous jars into which, time and time again, she would plunge loin cloths and tunics which were then put out to dry in the sun in the backyard of our house in Medina-Coura. My mother's hands and forearms were of an indigo colour too, like natural, indelible gloves.

'My sister, Dah, who was the eldest daughter in our family, used to go from market to market offering the cloth dyed by my mother to customers from nearby villages. The money they earned from this work went to supplement my father's income: he was a post office official. So I know better than anyone how the hands of women who create are also hands that feed.

'My "Little mother" – my father had several wives – in turn left a lasting impression on me. There was a strong bond of affection between us. It was she who taught me how to spin and embroider the white percale sheets that I used to sell for her at the main market in Bamako on Thursdays and Sundays when I didn't go to school. I can remember those long evenings when we used to spin the cotton while listening to tales and songs of former times. Memories of those days bring back a

variety of aromas such as incense and vetiver.

'My big sister, Dah, also left a lasting impression on my childhood. She has always been and still is my closest friend and accomplice. It was she who, throughout my schooldays, looked after me and provided me with pocket money, school stationery and clothes. I remain very grateful to her.

'Then came the time for me to get married, that transition to adulthood which, for women, is always experienced as a departure as they must leave their own family to join their husband's. The man I married, whom I separated from subsequently, came from Côte d'Ivoire. I therefore left my own country for a destination which, for me, became more than just a host country.

'I had perhaps changed countries but the atmosphere wasn't so different. My mother-in-law, Mah, also earned her living from manual work. She would spend hours and hours, with a long stick in her hand, stirring the boiling paste contained in large barrels, with which she used to make soap. My sisters-in-law used to sell these products at the Daloa market just as my sister and myself had done for our mother in Mali.

'The mammy-cloths I was given, as well as pocket money for my husband and other little treats we were entitled to as students, came from the proceeds of the sale of Mah's soap and occasionally palm oil.

'My studies in social psychology and psycho-pathology took me to France, to Caen, where my two daughters, Fatou and Awa, were born. Those years enabled me to discover other aspects of social and human reality and fostered deep nostalgia for the African continent. The period from 1969 to 1975 gave me an opportunity to step back and observe, which was very decisive for the task of reflection and creation on which I was to embark later on.

66

*AMINATA TRAORÉ'S WORKS SHOW
THAT THE AGE-OLD 'BOGOLAN' DESIGNS BY WOMEN IN
MALIAN VILLAGES ARE PERFECTLY SUITED
TO THE MOST CONTEMPORARY INTERIOR SETTINGS.*

'Once I had completed my doctorate in social psychology, I returned to Côte d'Ivoire and became a researcher at the Institute of Ethno-Sociology, which enabled me to explore social and economic conditions in the various regions of my country of adoption. When the Ministry for the Status of Women was set up in 1975, International Women's Year, I was put in charge of the Department of Studies and Curriculum and, as a member of that newly created department, I had an opportunity of travelling around the country, collecting quantitative and qualitative data on women.

'With responsibility for various projects, aimed at improving the circumstances and performance of women in certain sectors, including arts and crafts, I gradually became acquainted with such skills as the smoking of fish and the work of potters and I was able to witness the installation of kilns, smoke-rooms and other low-cost technologies.

'The long hours spent in the company of potters such as Baoulé and Mangoro while they fashioned their objects have left me with an unforgettable impression.

'Both in pottery as well as dyeing, a diversity of colours, shapes and functions struck me as being the only way to counter poor sales of women's handicrafts and the economic exclusion of craftswomen.

'When the United Nations Fund for Women asked me to study the circumstances of craftswomen in other African countries such as Mali, I was very glad of the opportunity to establish contact with potters in Mopti and Kalabougou, near Ségou.

'I have always been fascinated by the capacity for work and force of character of most of the craftswomen I have met. From them, I have learnt as much about the techniques and philosophy of their art as about the contradictions and aberrations of

what we are accustomed to calling development.

'However, I was no more than a link in a chain which stretched from New York, where funding decisions are taken, to Geneva where International Labour Organisation (ILO) experts are selected and to Abidjan and Bamako where national administrators have little or no choice but to give their support to projects put forward. Fed up with technical reports that led nowhere, I decided in 1984 to give free rein to my inspiration: I would no longer write about potters but would write for them and with them. At the same time, I opted definitively for a strategy based on listening and accompaniment.

'The promotion of potters, for example, did not depend merely on isolated solutions such as building kilns (largely ill-adapted and with poor performance levels) or processing clay. In addition to these improvements, account had to be taken of the domestic economic environment and the determination of politicians as well as the attitudes and behaviour of consumers.

'Why did political decision-makers see arts and crafts merely as an instrument for developing tourism, that is to say, a mere response to the demand and needs of others?

'We know all too well how recent experience has confirmed the failure of this model of outward-looking development. This same experience means that a new look has to be taken at art, arts and crafts and culture and the part they play in combating poverty and exclusion.

'The process on which I embarked through Djenné, San Toro and the Centre has enabled me to have a better understanding of how one can create and respond to the demands of other people, while remaining true to oneself.

'By introducing new forms and seeing to

67

SAHEL BASKET-WEAVERS USE
A UNIVERSAL TECHNIQUE
IN THE STYLE OF THEIR FOREBEARS.

it that their quality and finish remain up to standard, it is possible to create added value for products such as traditional cotton fabrics, earthenware and leather goods which the Africans themselves seem to have tired of in view of their unchanging style and declining quality.

'Today, Africans have no alternative but to create and invest in available resources. That alone can enable them to satisfy their own needs and make their presence felt on the international market.

'This undoubtedly raises the controversial issue of international standards and care must be taken to keep in tune with the needs of consumers, whether African or non-African. But it is just as important that Africa should set its own standards, establish its own trends and in turn exert its own influence on the market.

'Countries like ours must make the most of any opportunities that arise as we have a certain number of assets which have not all been fully exploited. However, such opportunities come and go and they must be correctly identified, developed and nurtured by those who have the inspiration and talent. Craftspeople, for their part, who have very little contact with the outside world and are not involved in comparing ideas and models, should be helped by creative artists.

'Chris Seydou, our talented fashion designer who died recently, had succeeded in making *bogolan*, traditional Malian handicrafts, some of the most sought-after products on the international fashion and interior design market in a context where the ecology-conscious consumer is also after natural products and dyes.

'The path I have followed as a researcher and an endogenous development activist has helped me considerably in my quest for other opportunities and in my creative activities.

Inspiration comes to me from the observation of materials. Then I plan the tasks to be carried out. Producing an object may involve several different trades, so close co-operation is established between craftspeople who do not usually work together. It is enriching both for them and for me.

'The work is carried out in the backyard or in one of the workshops at the Centre, but also in various buildings in Bamako or hinterland towns which are workshops for both craftsmen and craftswomen who are also housewives.

'The finished products are then displayed at San Toro which is our main outlet. Prospective customers ask us many questions about the objects and we endeavour to respond to their reactions and remarks. What I would like to do is to go more deeply into this kind of research/action work and to document it.

'My artistic and cultural activities have enabled me to establish close and very precious relationships with craftspeople. In economic terms, I have managed to create some forty permanent jobs and I employ several dozen people, some of whom work at home at their own pace and as they please, such as weavers who cannot move away from their usual place of work. Others work near me in a very convivial atmosphere; all are highly motivated and keen to ensure that the three establishments operate well. I try, as far as I can, to help them overcome their material and social problems.

'Within this particular structure, I find myself facing one of the most significant challenges of the late twentieth century: reconciling social development and economic profitability which is not always easy in poor countries where social needs are so great.

'Three members of my family help me, two of whom are conscientious administrators who may worry at times when I suddenly fall for a particular painting or valuable object or make

69

certain commitments as regards labour costs. Nevertheless, they trust my intuition and my attitude to money: while I recognize its importance, I should also like to rid it of its hold over people's minds.

'On the whole, all that has been achieved, in all modesty, at Djenné, San Toro and the Centre should contribute to producing new, original and sustainable solutions to development problems. Our countries' dependence on the outside world stems, first and foremost, from our own refusal to look at ourselves in a true light and to make judicious use of the existing wealth and solutions that are within our reach.

'Perhaps we have not been allowed sufficient leeway, yet it is up to us to express more firmly our desire to act responsibly.'

Traditional *ikat* weaving with Khun Na Saikeau and Khun Phian Saikeau

by Jasleen Dhamija

Bangkok

Throughout the world, the dyeing of textiles has always been a women's speciality. It's as if it were a secret cult in their society, governed by a system of taboos and ancestral rules. Women of the older generation have ruled over this process as if it were some occult, esoteric art: they preside at the dyeing ceremony like alchemists transforming raw silk and cotton into myriads of colours.

The most complex technique in this field is *mudmee* or *ikat*, whereby the warp and weft threads are first knotted and dyed so as to give a pattern to the weave. *Ikat* garments are considered to have a magic quality with the power to cure, protect and generate visionary qualities in weaver and wearer alike.

The art of using traditional dyes has long been closely linked to that of medicinal herbs, magic potions, secret poisons and fertility and virility drugs. Soaking the thread in dye baths according to the rites of the weather, the day, the seasons and the influence of the moon, keeping them out of daylight and protecting them from the forces of the subterranean world determine the hidden powers of these magic garments. The *ikat* technique, whereby the warp threads are brought together in hanks and bound in such a way as to form a motif apparent after the item has been dyed, has always been endowed with the power to cure and to protect but

also to destroy, if ever it is badly made.

The first step in making up the pattern involves tying the threads together so that they protect the basic white or pale yellow colour. The succession of ligatures on the intensity of the dyes increases the powers with which the garment is endowed and the complexity of the messages conveyed through its non-verbal expression.

Weaving is like breathing life into threads by creating a garment that reveals the whole of the pattern like hieroglyphs conveying a message to the initiated.

Over the centuries, these skills have been handed down exclusively to those who possessed appropriate spiritual, psychic and intellectual aptitudes as well as physical and mental purity. Not only manual agility and a particular aesthetic sense but also a strong personality and considerable dexterity are required to break down a pattern into its basic components at the tying stage before reconstituting it when the warp is placed on the loom and through the movement of the weft that weaves the garment.

The weave patterns are produced within a complex frame which itself determines a sacred area. It is within this frame that the abstract motif is produced. Women have always made one type of garment for daily use and another for special occasions.

KHUN PHIAN SAIKEAU IN HER WORKSHOP
PATIENTLY TIES THE SILK THREADS
OF A CHAIN TO WEAVE A
'PHASIN' (WOMAN'S SARONG).
BEHIND HER HANGS A 'PHA BIANG'
(WOMAN'S SASH).

74

KHUN NA SAIKEAU, MASTER-WEAVER

OF 'MUDMEE HOLLE'

(RITUAL CEREMONIAL DRESS), IS FAITHFUL

TO TRADITION AND IS HANDING DOWN

HER CRAFT TO HER DAUGHTER.

To the lay person, this act of creation is an ordinary craft whereas, to the initiated, it has a much stronger meaning which, quite often, the craftswomen themselves are unable to define. They therefore offer a banal explanation according to which they forgot the real meaning a long time ago or they do not wish to reduce the garment's special powers by talking about it.

Nevertheless, if you work with them for a while, observe the various processes and follow the rituals that accompany each phase – and are often practised without understanding their true significance – up to when the garment is finally used, its hidden meaning will come to light.

Khun Na Saikeau, a master-weaver of great renown, lives in Ban Nacheeuw, a small village in the Surin area in north-eastern Thailand. It's a Thai Khmer village. Two of her daughters live with her together with their husbands and children, in accordance with regional tradition whereby a young man settles in his wife's village and lives with her family.

Her youngest daughter, Phian, learned the art of making silk from her mother: gathering, unwinding, knotting, dyeing and weaving. She is now carrying on the art of the powerful *mudmee holle* based on plant dyes.

Traditionally, every man and woman must have two *mudmee holle* that they wear on every ceremonial occasion.

Khun Na Saikeau is now 80 years old and continues to spend her days winding the silk on the old wooden spinning wheel carved by her last husband.

Sitting on a wooden bench at the bottom of her garden, with her children and grandchildren around her, she winds the woven silk while keeping an attentive eye on the indigo vats and the fabrics that have been put outside in front of another house.

This is where she receives visitors and where I met her.

On that particular day, she called her daughter and neighbours and asked them, 'Sing her the *chareang mudmee* (the *ikat* costume song) so that she can repeat the words to people all over the world'.

And the singer began: '*Hun hun*' . . . '*Oey oey*' . . . while Khun Na nodded gently and smiled and the noise of her spinning wheel echoed in response.

'Listen, listen everybody!
I asked my grandmother
I asked my grandfather
I asked the whole world
For permission to sing
To sing this song.
Hun hun Oey oey
Those who want to clad themselves in silk
Must discover
Yes, they must discover everything
About our *mudmee*
Our two sorts of *mudmee*
Mudmee sin and *mudmee holle*
Which have so many colours
Oh ever so many colours of truth
Colours that sing
Only those who are pure
Only those who are truthful
May wear our silk *mudmees*.
We unwind the pure, shining silk
From the slumbering silkworms.
We unwind the long threads
We spin the short threads
And colour with our hearts
And colour with our minds
Hun hun Oey oey
Chat chat Oey oey.'

Khun Na's spinning wheel had stopped, she was far away, in another world: 'I was 9 when my grandmother began to teach me. It was she who taught me that song while she spun the thread on her spinning wheel, unwound the silk, prepared the thread and wove it. It was only when she was busy with the dyeing that we had to keep quiet. Even the forest fell silent then, especially when we used indigo. The spirit of indigo does not enter the vat if it is disturbed. When we approached the *mhou nin*, a blue sapphire jar, we had to concentrate our whole being.'

Khun Na laughed gently and, putting a finger on her lips, whispered, *Lucknee kui mhou nin*, and the spirit disappeared as if it had been there one moment and gone the next.

'One of my earliest childhood memories was waiting for the rain to fall after the *songkran*, our New Year. It is a period of rest, celebrations and festivities when we go to the temple. But I was always impatient as, after all that, we would start breeding the silkworms. We had to scrub the big tables and the canvass that covered them so as to keep the flies away. I also had to clean the clay bowls in which the table trestles stood so that ants could not climb up. Soon after the end of the month, all was ready and the eggs were put carefully into a basket which we kept in a warm place so that they would hatch. The tiny worms would come out and we would feed them with small pieces of mulberry leaves. The first thing my grandmother ever taught me was how to pick young shoots and cut them up into small pieces for the young silkworms. They soon began to grow and I would help my grandmother pick out the most vigorous ones so as to put them into a larger round basket, the *kradang*. She would put the worms onto the palms of my hands and say "tender hand of a child, carry them gently". For me, it was a game and a way of keeping close to my grandmother. I had never known my mother who had died when I was very young.

'I owe everything I know to my grandmother. It was she who taught me how to work with the *mudmee holle* when I was 14, at a time when men would come to our garden to sing to us. "I'm teaching you all this very early because I don't know how long I have still to live", she would say.

'One of the first important things I had to learn were the rules to be observed if I wanted to learn the art of the *mudmee holle*. I have to have great powers of concentration, my thoughts should focus on my grandmother who taught me everything and on my teacher's teacher, my great-grandmother who trained them all a long time ago. I must be pure, in body and soul, otherwise the pure spirit of the *mudmee holle* might leave me, the spirit of indigo gnaw away at me and the ants that were used to make the indigo colour set might come and eat me up in the night. Nor must I let myself be weakened by illness or menstruation. I must remain strong in mind and body. When the master is ill, we should not weave. Likewise, whenever there is a death in the house, the looms stop for a week.'

She called her youngest daughter, Phian, and had her sit down beside her. 'Although she's the youngest, it's Phian to whom I've passed on my skills. My grandmother and her ancestors would certainly have approved as I know that Phian will succeed in keeping this family tradition alive and, as long as she follows the right path, our family will be prosperous and never be short of rice, even if nature is not always very bountiful.

'You ought really to ask Phian these questions as she is the one who practises this craft now. It was she who flew off to a remote country where, they tell me, they sent men to the moon and back. It wasn't just a flying machine that carried Phian off but also the living spirit of indigo.'

Phian listens quietly to her mother while

unwinding a thread for her. Yes, she went to school because Khun Na wanted her to learn to read and write, but she left when she was 14. She shows us all the books that have been written on her work and proudly describes her trip to Washington at the invitation of the Smithsonian Institution.

Khun Na, Phian and her sister live together on the same plot of land, in the company of their husbands and children and those of another aunt. They live close to nature where life follows the rhythm of the seasons. Their dyed woven silk fabrics are also in perfect harmony with nature.

The month before the monsoon is one of rest. It is a time when they venerate their ancestors and go on pilgrimages and there is much singing and dancing. However, preparations have to be made for the very busy period of rice planting. The women who feed the silkworms must make sure that everything is ready in order to satisfy the growing appetite of the worms during the last days before they begin to spin their cocoons. They then have to be fed day and night, leaving the family very little time for sleep.

The preparation of indigo (*Indigo fera tinctura*), known locally as *khram,* will also begin. Local tradition has it that it must be planted before the first croaks of the bullfrogs, that is to say, before the rainy season, and that it must be cut before the mists appear, that is to say, the end of the rainy season. The paste is prepared with cut leaves and put into the old vats which have often been in the family for many years.

The red colour is obtained from shellac (*Coccus lacca*), known here as *krang*; it is the secretion of a female insect, found on the branches of the rain tree (*Samanea saman*).[*]

---

[*] See Susan Conway, *Thai Textiles,* Bangkok, Asian Book Company, 1992.

The yellow colour comes from two types of wood, one being probably the bark of a tree (*Rauw enhoffa siamensis*) and the other, the core of the mulberry tree or Jack tree.

During the rainy season, the women make the materials they will need for their weaving but also lend a hand in the fields.

The weaving period starts as soon as the harvest has been brought in; the breeding of the cocoons is then over and these are gathered and stored.

While the men can at last relax once the harvest is over, the women begin the tasks of unwinding the silk and removing any glue, and then knotting the threads so as to make the five-coloured garments which accompany every man and woman from birth until death. The *phasin* or silk sarong for women is produced according to a type of striped *ikat*, which resembles bamboo leaves. The sarong is worn with a scarf across the shoulder, the *pha biang* which, for women, has a particular pattern of stippled losanges and the *mudmee*. For men, the pattern is diamond-shaped and the scarf much longer so that it can be gathered in between the legs.

This work requires exceptional skill in knotting and dyeing the thread to form the pattern. It is this particular technique that Phian has mastered with such talent under the guidance of Khun Na. First, the white threads are knotted on those parts that are to remain white, yellow or pale blue. The hank of the warp knotted in this way is then immersed in the red dye (lac).

Once the desired shade of red has been obtained, the part that is to remain red is then knotted in the same way as those parts that are to become dark blue.

During the next phase, the white threads that are to be yellow are untied at the same time as those that will veer to green, and are then immersed in the yellow dye.

78

CLOSE-UP OF PATTERN OF A MAN'S 'PHA BIANG'
WORN DURING THE RITES OF PASSAGE.
THE FIVE COLOURS REPRESENT
THE FIVE ELEMENTS AND THE FAVOURABLE
INFLUENCE OF THE PLANETS.

When removed from the vat, the parts that are to remain yellow are knotted once again and the white sections that are supposed to acquire a pale blue colour are opened with the red sections that will become bluish black.

The threads are then soaked in indigo for the last, decisive time.

When they are removed and exposed to the air, an assortment of bright colours appears. The effect of the indigo intensifies, the whites become pale blue, the reds veer to dark blue and the yellow mixed with blue turns green.

The fabric is finally removed from the vat and the ligatures are unknotted.

The soaking in three stages produces a multitude of different shades of white, yellow, green, red, light blue and dark blue.

This is the *mudmee holle* weaving technique, so difficult to master, and for which the first UNESCO Prize for Creativity was awarded at the Arts and Crafts of Asia competition in 1992.

The *pha biang*, with a similar style of stripes, is produced with a multi-coloured weft, the threads of which are of the five colours of the rainbow: purple, green, yellow, deep pink and white, representing the five elements and the favourable influence of the planets. The *pha biang* is also a source of strength in initiation rites.

The new-born child, for example, is wrapped in his parents' old clothes, among which the five-coloured *mudmee holle* is the most remarkable. Mother and child are also confined for seven days to a room where a fire is kept alight and where special garments such as the *mudmee holle* are hung around them to protect them.

During their preparation for initiation, young novices wear the *pha biang* and the five-coloured *mudmee holle* and only remove them when they don the ascetic's robe. Similarly, in funereal rites, the *pha biang* is left on the coffin until incineration begins but it is not thrown into the flames but given back to the family after purification, so that it may be used by the next generation. That is why this particular item must be crafted with intense concentration by virtue of the strength it imparts and its ritual meaning.

In Africa, weaving is normally men's work as they are responsible for protecting the family from the elements and life's dangers. Here, in South-East Asia, it is the women who weave as they are thought to provide human society with nourishment and preserve it from malevolent influences. It is the women who are closest to nature and derive from its resources the deeply rooted strength to protect the family and society as a whole.

Khun Na Saikeau and her daughter Phian have succeeded in preserving this tradition that draws its resources from nature and is in close harmony with the rhythm of the seasons and their fruit.

They have never succumbed to the temptation of using chemical dyes which might have given them a wider market and simpler methods of production. Their skills, talent and devotion to this art remain profound and authentic.

The craftspeople around them, who have witnessed their success, have gone back to using plant dyes.

Mother and daughter have therefore nurtured and consolidated the traditions of their people and its capacity to lead a rich and meaningful life.

Sadika Kammoun: rebirth of a glass-blowing tradition

by Hamma Hanachi

82

The breath of life

Soon after independence, education in Tunisia was widely democratized, as schools, colleges and specialized institutes sprang up everywhere. Most young people were able to go to school and boys and girls sat side by side in the classroom, even in the most remote villages, and shared the same ambition and nurtured the same hopes of pursuing their studies as far as possible and gaining access to a good job.

This educational policy, combined with that of improving the status of women, has proved successful and produced surprising results.

Encouraged by more egalitarian relations and protected by the 'code of personal status', Tunisian women gradually gained access to many social and professional spheres, taking up positions in the civil service, at the bar, at universities and in business. What is more, women have been successful in some traditionally masculine trades.

Sadika Kammoun is a perfect example of a woman who has had a successful career over the last few decades. In point of fact she is a virtually unique case that clearly illustrates the degree of feminine emancipation in Tunisian society and reflects its development and achievements.

Her own experience and success are by no means negligible as many lessons can be drawn from them, inasmuch as they have revived a craft that was hitherto forgotten and neglected in Tunisian society.

The craft of glass-blowing, as practised by Sadika, lost its living roots in Tunisia many centuries ago.

Within easy walking distance of the sea, in the suburbs of Tunis, in Gammarth (formerly Megara) near Carthage, now a major tourist site, is a blue and white workshop built in the Arab architectural tradition with blue wrought iron on the façade and three small domes crowning the roof.

The workshop, which has a surface area of 350 square metres, comprises areas for glass-blowing and decoration of objects as well as a spacious exhibition hall.

The workshop is always buzzing with Tunisian or foreign visitors, tourists and patrons from nearby hotels. While some visitors examine a phial in one corner, others admire a vase in another, whilst still others observe the young apprentices working at the table and attempt to satisfy their curiosity by questioning them on the decoration, materials and objects.

The owner and founder of the workshop is Sadika Kammoun, a woman who runs her business with remarkable rigour. She is in fact

IN SADIKA'S WORKSHOP

NEAR CARTHAGE,

THE WONDER OF GLASS-BLOWING

AND THE CREATION OF SHAPES

THAT CATCH THE LIGHT.

the first woman to practise the reputedly exacting craft of glass-blowing.

Sadika would like her workshop to be just like the interior of a Tunisian house where visitors may feel they are guests of a Tunisian family, talking of this and that and discussing the various objects, their shapes and colours, over a glass of tea.

Apprenticeship

When she was 14, at secondary school, Sadika happened to take part in an international drawing competition. She won a prize that persuaded her to follow an artistic career.

She describes it as an important event and a turning-point. In 1979, Sadika passed her baccalaureate in maths and science. She then enrolled at the Technological Institute of Art, Architecture and Town-Planning in Tunis where she studied the fine arts for four years in the Department of Plastic Arts.

As to her reason for choosing this speciality, no doubt it was by chance: but chance can also be fashioned and developed through love of what one does and the desire to do it well. As daughter and granddaughter of cabinet-makers (her grandfather was 'Lamine', head of the guild of cabinet-makers in Sfax), she says: 'I think that the love of materials comes partly from my origins and partly from the context in which I grew up, a family of craftsmen who talked constantly about form and design and discussed various processes and methods that inspired in me a profound respect for this craft. . . .'

In 1981 she went to Italy to do a course in glass-making techniques in Murano, with the Seguso Vetri d'Arte company, returning there in 1982 to do a similar course.

In 1983, she was one of a group of glass-blowing artists who exhibited at the Information Gallery in Tunis. Her tastes were taking shape and she went back to Murano for

a third time in 1983 to do another course in the same Italian city.

She came back full of hope and nurtured on new experience and decided to open her first glass-blowing workshop. She was then caught up in a quite singular commercial venture, working tirelessly, moulding glass and inventing new shapes. She also assimilated a variety of techniques and styles. Her workshop was soon to become too small as the objects she created gradually filled all the shelves, tables and floor space.

She dreamt of finding more spacious premises and was able to find the support she needed, both direct and indirect, material and moral, from the Ministry of Tourism and Arts and Crafts. 'In that tiny workshop, I used to work well into the night. A television crew from FR2 who had come to film my work were astonished, almost shocked, to see me blowing glass when I was eight months pregnant. They probably couldn't understand my determination to succeed and the joy I experienced when battling with the materials and the shapes. It was no doubt an expression of my own anxiety. . . .'

Background

In 1989 Sadika was awarded the Prize for Creation in Arts and Crafts. Hand in hand with her creative work, she began research on glass and submitted a dissertation in order to obtain a 'Certificat d'Aptitude à la Recherche'.

A particular feature of her career has always been the constant combination of theoretical research and creative activity. In 1991 she was awarded the Prize for Creation in Arts and Crafts for the second time. The following year she was involved in a group exhibition entitled 'Plastic Space' as part of a university cultural programme. The works of that particular period were of very different aesthetic origins: Venetian, Czech and other

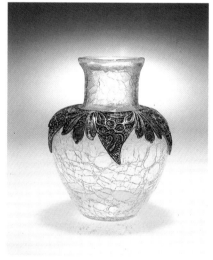

IN HER LATEST WORKS,
SADIKA EXPLORES THE USE OF
OTHER MATERIALS (SILVER CHAINS,
CHISELLED 'KHOMSA',
OR HAMMERED METAL)
IN RELATION TO THE CRYSTALLINE CLARITY
OR OPALINE DENSITY OF THE GLASS.

ABOVE: THE BIGGEST CHANDELIER IN
THE WORLD (15,000 BULBS OF BLOWN GLASS)
LIGHTS THE HALL OF A DJERBA HOTEL.
BELOW: SADIKA DISPLAYS THE ASTONISHING VARIETY
OF HER WORK IN HER WORKSHOP-CUM-SHOP.

sources. It was on the basis of this particular heterogeneous, ill-defined range of symbols that she produced her different objects.

She continued to take part in various competitions and, in 1992 and again in 1995, won the Prize for Creation in Arts and Crafts, a reference for amateurs and creators of artistic and craft objects.

Her technical and theoretical training prompted her to adopt a very personal approach which lies within the compass of the Arab heritage and draws inspiration from it.

'Glass-blowing should not merely be the automatic reproduction of works from the past; our tradition, once it has been acquired, should enable us to understand the present. I have therefore used as my starting-point the earlier forms which I attempt to update, particularly in terms of form (function) and materials (cost and colour).

'Any exponents of the plastic arts, who are conscious of what their work represents, should express their identity by endeavouring to lend a modern, contemporary interpretation to their heritage. . . .'

In the meantime, Sadika was invited to teach drawing and glass-blowing at the School of Fine Arts, and embarked on research to prepare a thesis on the introduction of Bohemian and Venetian glass-blowing in the eighteenth and nineteenth centuries.

The art of glass-blowing in Tunisia can boast of a remarkable history, to say the least. The origins of the craft are virtually lost in the mists of time, in the Punic and Carthaginian eras. Archaeological excavations conducted in the Carthaginian cities have brought to light many glass objects which now belong to the Tunisian museum collections. Evidence of glass-making in Carthaginian culture has been confirmed by the remains of workshops and kilns in Carthage and Kerkouene.

The Roman period too had a rich glass-blowing tradition: objects were made using two techniques, i.e. with and without a mould. Vases, cinerary urns and utensils as illustrated in numerous mosaics, paintings and frescoes testify to the Roman mastery of glass-making.

Glass-making continued during the Arab period and many glass factories have been discovered dating back to the Fatimid, Zirid and Hammadid periods. 'In the Eastern Berber region, glassware was manufactured for various purposes. At Mahdia, Sabra and Kairouan, the Fatimids used objects made of molten and stamped glass. At Qal'a, fragments have also been found of phials, handles, bottlenecks and receptacle bases sometimes decorated with intaglio engraving. Most of the glass fragments are white but some are peacock blue, green or red. All these items, of which the remaining fragments are very incomplete, are usually very small, but they do prove that glass-making was a common activity in the towns of Ifriqia.'

Curiously enough, the art of glass-making disappeared in Tunisia for several centuries.

During the eighteenth and nineteenth centuries, many glassware items were imported from Bohemia, and this was the subject of Sadika's thesis on techniques in arts and crafts.

Adaptation of this glassware to the tastes and traditions of an oriental clientele can be detected via the trading networks through which they reached Tunisia (Turkey, Egypt as well as direct routes). Subsequently, Sadika Kammoun intends to undertake practical research on glass-making for which glass imported from Bohemia, considered as part of

* G. Marçais and P. Poinsot, with L. Gaillard, *Objets Kairouanais du IXe au XIXe siècle: reliures, verreries, cuivres, bronzes et bijoux,* Tunis/Paris, Éditions Tournier/ Klincksieck.

the Tunisian heritage, would constitute, in both technical as well as aesthetic terms, a source of inspiration which could lead to original, new creations, although deeply rooted in their authenticity.

Consecration

There are influences of a remote heritage in what Sadika Kammoun produces, and her creations draw on the national heritage as well as universal inventions. Her work, which initially was a sort of theoretical premeditation applied to materials and took the form of a range of highly skilled exercises, gradually changed substantially. 'Glass-blowing', she confides, 'is not a craft to be cultivated by chance but must take account of what a given culture needs. In the early days, when I was learning my craft, I was certainly influenced by foreign products and objects, mainly of Venetian origin; I even made copies of them. It was probably because I was producing a lot that I did not escape criticism in some quarters.'

Today, Sadika works with the spatial dimension just as a sculptor does; there is a succession and interpenetration of humps and hollows that give the material the desired, final shape. Sometimes the addition of other materials, such as silver chains, chiselled *khomsa* or hammered metal (more frequent in her latest creations) appear and can be seen as embellishments that bring the design to life and the specificity of the materials in relation to the crystalline clarity or opaline density of the glass. A profusion of geometrical or animal motifs, according to the stylized Tunisian tradition, appears on carafes and jars, transparent or opaque glass dishes with chiselled or filigree silver embellishments and a series of clogs moulded and blown in clear glass 'which have proved very popular among foreign customers', according to Sadika.

How has this change come about and does it reflect a break with tradition or a natural development?

'Today, I devote my time solely to creation. This break is undoubtedly due to nty greater theoretical and practical skills, to contact with other creators and, in a nutshell, a new vision of the world. Besides that, I've broken free from the burden of daily chores. A few years ago, my work was too disorganized as I had to look after running the company with all that entails in the way of chores such as appointments with customers, orders, bills, negotiating with retailers and running the home. . . .'

Does this mean that her family life has suffered? 'Not at all,' she says, 'but I've learnt how to organize my life according to my work and I've managed to reconcile my life as an artist and craftswoman with that of a mother. As you can see, there are a number of assistants in my workshop whom I've trained, apprentices who do the finishing work. In the past I used to do everything from start to finish, all alone.

'Another important aspect of my life is the total absence of any timetable. I devote whatever time I please to my children and I work when I set about inventing a new line, a new form or when I have urgent orders to meet . . . .'

It has been a long time since Sadika had to battle alone on all fronts as her tenacity, combined with considerable energy, have overcome those difficulties.

'I was faced with difficulties from the very start as I didn't have a workshop because the craft of glass-blowing just didn't exist. It took me a year to bring together what I needed and to build my first kiln. At the time, I took on two apprentices to help me but I had the financial problems entailed in maintaining a kiln for glass-blowing. I went five years without making any profit.'

The results, however, were not long in coming. Glass objects produced in her workshop began to be displayed in hotel shops and handicraft galleries and then found their way into the drawing rooms and display cabinets of private houses. Orders poured in.

'I had to wait eight years before obtaining authorization to open my workshop in the tourist district of Gammarth where I am now. The Minister of Tourism and Handicrafts himself, convinced that my project was worthwhile, had to intervene on my behalf. It must be said, of course, that my project was the first of its kind, a pilot project which could raise various problems such as feasibility, profitability and so forth. The lack of understanding I met from some people inspired me, as it sometimes does, with determination to fight and gave me the energy I needed to achieve my aims. . . .'

In the meantime, Sadika continued to win prizes and was invited to exhibit her products abroad. In 1993, she took part in the International Salon du PAAS in Paris and also exhibited some of her work at the Frankfurt International Fair.

The French stylist, Christian Lacroix, well-known for his desire to encourage the combination of different cultures, commissioned objects from her and these creations won acclaim from public and critics alike.

In 1994, she produced a chandelier with the largest number of bulbs in the world for a hotel in Djerba and applied to have this certified in the *Guinness Book of Records.*

Does all this success make her proud?

'Yes, in part, as these achievements do represent an element of success. But what gives me the greatest satisfaction is training young glass-blowers. Ever since I began, my aim has been to ensure that this profession was revived in Tunisia. What gives me satisfaction is to acknowledge that there are young apprentices who are very interested in the work and, within a few years, I'm sure that other workshops will open and the profession will have the place it deserves. . . .'

What is a typical day like in the life of Sadika, craftswoman and mother?

'Fortunately, every day is different and many things have changed in my life. Years ago, in my old workshop, I used to spend roughly eight months a year glass-blowing, between five and six days a week. If I have managed to be entirely free today to use my time as I please, it's also thanks to the understanding attitude of my husband who always believed in what I was doing. He is the one who runs the company today and markets my products while, when I'm in the workshop, I can devote myself completely to "creative work". I stand in front of the lighted kiln with tongues and scissors in my hand and tackle the molten glass, trying to transform it. It can sometimes take nights on end so I leave instructions to the apprentices who decorate the objects (often in front of visitors).

'Teaching matters a lot to me and takes up a large part of my time. Encouraging students to take an interest in glass-blowing is a noble task, I believe. Add to that the task of bringing up the children, plus any unexpected event, and you have a pretty full day. . . .'

Here lies the core of Sadika's experience which – above and beyond the plastic qualities of her works, the rigour of her approach and the masterly coherence of a life completely devoted to the love of her profession – brings a new dimension into play.

According to the contemporary axiom by which the signature makes the work, then glass-blowing as a craft is the expression of an individual, and craft objects become true works of art.

Carolyn McKecuen and Watermark: a model association of craftspeople

by Caroline Ramsay

Washington

Carolyn McKecuen is a talented potter and is also the Executive Director of the Watermark Association of Artisans, one of the largest co-operatives in the United States, having 750 members. Carolyn McKecuen's story reveals how she has used crafts as a vehicle for personal success, for the professional enhancement of rural women and for the economic development of the areas where they work.

Watermark is the single largest employer in Camden County, North Carolina, and offers various levels of employment in a county where few jobs are available for women and pay is at a minimum. Besides paying fair wages, Watermark offers flexible hours. Since women can work at home, they do not have to hire baby-sitters, buy working clothes or have travelling expenses. They can work as many hours as they wish. Watermark provides training so that a person can become employed sometimes with only a few hours of instruction. This gives people a chance to start making money quickly in order to cope with emergencies.

Moreover, Watermark's training centre, the North-Eastern Education and Development Foundation (NEED), has set up a $45,000 loan fund that enables women to buy supplies and equipment. Consequently, the members of the co-operative – mostly women – can become economically independent.

'A woman's place in the business world is any place where she has the competence, persistence and desire to be', says Carolyn, who has lived in this area for over twenty years and has seen for herself the great need for an enterprise like Watermark. It is an example of what poor rural people, largely women, can accomplish through a highly organized co-operative crafts project.

Carolyn feels that women who believe in themselves 'can create their own destiny'. She has certainly fostered a successful destiny for her organization and her region. In 1994, she was awarded the prestigious MacArthur Fellowship Award for the most talented creators. She has also received other awards such as that for the Distinguished Women of North Carolina.

Earlier, in 1993, she worked in Russia with students and women's organizations within the context of the US Agency for International Development and, in 1991, conducted workshops in Budapest for Hungarian women entrepreneurs.

In the United States, she taught pottery for several years at Albemarle College in North Carolina, where she had previously owned a crafts gallery. Mention should also be made of all the initiatives to which she has lent her

CAROLYN MCKECUEN
IN HER
WATERMARK OFFICE.

94

ABOVE: BUILDINGS OF THE WATERMARK
CO-OPERATIVE IN CAMDEN COUNTY.
BELOW: THE WATERMARK STORES OFFER A BROAD SPECTRUM
OF CRAFT PRODUCTS FROM THE ENTIRE REGION.

support in this region as well as in Tennessee, Georgia and Pennsylvania, particularly with the Artisans' Co-operatives.

While continuing to manage Watermark, Carolyn also works for NEED, the training centre she established in 1986 and which her husband, George McKecuen, directs today. Within the Watermark National Business Internship Program, she conducts workshops and seminars on various business topics. As a consultant or 'resource person', she has worked in Somalia and Tanzania to help create co-operatives, and New York and Washington, D.C., where she has been involved in assistance projects for various bodies and foundations.

Largely because of Carolyn's vision, craft talents, energy, business expertise and commitment to social justice, Watermark today is known world-wide for developing employment opportunities for unskilled workers.

The co-operative provides not only a source of much-needed income for rural women in North Carolina but a sense of self-esteem and accomplishment. Watermark's members live within a fifty-mile radius of Camden. A thriving enterprise, it is actually the only non-farming business in Camden County, a county so small that it has only one traffic light and so poor that the average income for a family of four does not exceed $20,000.

Watermark serves a 250-square-mile area made up of fifteen counties with only 200,000 inhabitants, three-quarters of whom are white and the rest primarily African American. Watermark's new 10,000-square-foot building houses a colourful, attractively organized two-storey retail store, an office complex, a training centre and a wholesale packaging and shipping area.

Traditionally, Camden has been a farming community, though some of its inhabitants worked in nearby shipyards and factories. Farming was a risky, low-profit business and the shipyards and factories were laying many people off. Things were not easy in this north-eastern corner of the state where annual incomes hovered around the poverty line. Carolyn discovered the area, where she now lives, in 1981 and witnessed the endless cycles of poverty and hopelessness. She decided to try and change things. She left her job as pottery instructor at the local community college, closed down her workshop and set about turning Watermark around.

Today, fourteen years later, Watermark is a thriving business which features two distinct product lines: country crafts and gift accessories. The country crafts range from rustic folk art to contemporary folk art via Victorian styles. The gift accessories comprise painted buttons, intricately carved wooden pieces and fine household linen items. Its decoratively painted wooden products, textiles, quilts, ceramics, rag dolls, stuffed bears, decoys, baskets and wreaths are sold to over 4,000 shops, department store chains and mail-order companies throughout the world.

Watermark is also capable of responding to special orders, ranging from single items to 46,000 units of a particular product.

It concludes contracts with companies to produce part of a product such as the stuffing and finishing of pillows, the weaving and embroidery of which are done in Hungary, Jordan and other countries, or to manufacture various national flags for the 1996 Olympic Games in Atlanta.

This helps foreign companies with their distribution and provides more work, income and goodwill for Watermark.

Who, in point of fact, are the Watermark producers?

They fall into three categories: the

95

96

ABOVE: ALL THE CO-OPERATIVE CRAFTSPEOPLE

WORK AT HOME AT THEIR OWN PACE.

BELOW: IN ADDITION, THEY ALL CONTRIBUTED

A PATTERN TO THIS TAPESTRY IN THE WATERMARK OFFICE.

'hobbyists' (approximately 400) who sell their production through the Watermark retail outlets; the members of the co-operative (approximately 200) who work for retailers and wholesalers; and 100 artisans. Most of these producers have been recruited by word of mouth, a brochure mailed by Watermark or the media. They have been chosen according to the quality of three of their products by a Screening and Jurying Committee.

Watermark's spectacular development over the last thirteen years has been largely due to setting more ambitious objectives, greater diversification of sales, short- and long-term business plans and emphasis on wholesaling.

After generating most of its income through retail sales at its local shop, Carolyn McKecuen began to concentrate on the wholesale business. She started with short merchandizing trips to New York.

'When my husband would take a business trip to New York, I would talk him into driving instead of flying so I could go along with a load of items from the co-operative.' In New York, Carolyn would sell Watermark crafts to retailers in wholesale lots of a dozen or so. Gradually she began to do this at gift shows. Soon, wholesale orders began to grow. 'Instead of sitting in the cornfield and waiting for buyers to come to us, we were going after them on the wholesale market.'

Today, Watermark produces a high-quality multicolour catalogue which is sent to 27,000 customers, sells at most gift shops throughout the country, and does special orders for national and international organizations like the Smithsonian Institution, Save the Children Fund and Aid to Artisans or for brands such as Neiman Marcus, Esprit and Ralph Lauren.

Watermark catalogue operations began when Carolyn asked women to bring in mail-order catalogues they were receiving. She then sent the companies samples or photographs of Watermark crafts and followed that up with letters. 'I read magazines like the *Italics Craft Report* and *Gift and Decorative Accessories*. Every time I would see a shop that had opened up, I would give them a call, send them pictures of our products and just hound them.'

In recent years, sales have been increased by marketing through the QVC cable television channel and by large-volume orders such as those for Ralph Lauren and Esprit. At present, 94 per cent of Watermark's business is wholesale.

Watermark has also been largely responsible for certain changes in demand and market trends. Carolyn stresses that 'you have to be one step ahead of the rest of the world'.

Although sales volume has gained steadily over the past decade, the net margins of the craft industry are small. Watermark's promise of prompt delivery and high-quality crafts, together with its marketing abilities, have enabled it to compete successfully with low-wage markets in Thailand, the Philippines, Hong Kong, Taiwan and China. Nevertheless, competitive pressure on Watermark to maintain low prices conflicts with its wish to pay its artisans prices in keeping with their time and effort.

This dilemma makes it necessary to uphold co-operative principles amongst members of the organization in order to ensure, over and above mere profit, that women in rural areas enjoy a measure of education and autonomy based on self-employment.

For the same reason, training plays an important part in Watermark's overall approach. When NEED was set up in 1986, the aim was to develop and adapt the talents of artisans so that they could meet company standards. Training has been devised on global

97

98

lines and each new member is assigned to a 'Watermark-buddy', a Watermark member who produces in the same medium as the trainee and can answer questions about organization and production. Meetings are held several times a year for each craft medium so that old and new members alike can discuss problems, share production ideas and be sure that everyone is conforming to a design, materials and production techniques on which they have all agreed.

Courses in business skills train members to read and understand financial statements and learn about accounting procedures, US business regulations and micro-enterprise lending. Workshops are conducted on market research, wholesale and retail systems, television marketing, trade fairs, promotional techniques and long-term planning, among other subjects.

In order to make the training accessible to all, there are classes at night as well as during the day and scholarships are awarded to trainees who cannot pay.

A significant part of this training is aimed at personal development, self-assurance and self-confidence, especially for women from disheartened and over-pessimistic homes.

According to Carolyn, training should emphasize 'life skills' as well as business and job skills.

Carolyn McKecuen, a driving force

This friendly, enthusiastic 50-year-old does not seem, in the words of Anne Lowrey Bailey, 'like a corporate executive or a saviour of the poor . . . but a cross between Donald Trump and Mother Teresa. She has built one of America's largest craft co-operatives in one of North Carolina's poorest counties and has trained low-income women to make money out of handmade crafts that have flourished in this region for centuries'.

Born and bred in Winston-Salem, North Carolina, Carolyn does not hide the fact that she once wanted to be a nun. Later, when she set her sights on crafts, her father tried to discourage her by warning her that she had no artistic skills. But she took this as a challenge and decided to become a potter. She still creates a few ceramic pieces, several of which decorate her office. She is also a caricaturist and her drawings are to be found in the offices of many associates and friends.

She likes meeting a challenge. For instance, when she heard someone say that 'women cannot sky-dive', she enrolled in a parachute-jumping school to prove him wrong and 'even though I hate planes, I've jumped several times'.

She moved to Camden in 1974 with her husband who taught at a local college. She opened her own workshop there and set up a craft-marketing business. Faced along with another co-operative with a debt of $16,000, she took things in hand and, in 1981, began to make changes. She shared out difficulties between various associates, began developing more marketable products, enlarged the membership base and decided to emphasize wholesaling rather than retailing. She succeeded in revitalizing Watermark and the community that surrounds it and earned herself the MacArthur Fellowship. As Mary Mountcastle, President of the Board of the Smith Reynolds Foundation, observes: 'Carolyn sees her marketplace as the world, and not just the twenty miles around where she is located. For low-income women in that region, Watermark is their link with the global economy'.

Now, thanks to the MacArthur Fellowship funds, Carolyn is helping many other co-operatives in the area, extending the NEED training programme by recruiting women in local home projects and increasing the flow of people who visit Watermark to learn more about it.

Carolyn hopes that Watermark will serve as a model and that its experience will help other individuals and groups in the United States and overseas. She is ready to offer them her assistance and is also planning to write a book. In the meantime, she would like to take a vacation with her husband, their first in fourteen years, and finish paying off some personal debts that accumulated while they took minimal pay at Watermark.

Carolyn's office is cluttered with objects, a colourful assortment of all sorts of craft products. On one wall there is a large quilt composed of squares made by each member, each depicting what Watermark means to them. Artisans and staff members come in and out and the telephone rings constantly. Nearby, artisans are making shirts, caps, mugs and kits for a Ms. Foundation programme in which Watermark is involved. Girls aged 9 to 15 accompany their parents in order to discuss their work and write about their experience. In the kitchen, other staff members bake hand-painted jam pots to make sure the paint sets before starting a run of some 90,000 pieces for the Silvestri Corporation.

The enormous publicity which Watermark has received can be seen in the multitude of clippings on the walls throughout the building. It has also been featured countless times on television programmes. It is clear that Carolyn is very proud of Watermark.

This success can be attributed to her determination, hard work, research and common sense approach. She knows perfectly how to base production on careful market analysis. No product is actually made until an order has been received. Those orders are then given to the artisans with specific deadlines for each product, usually two to three months before delivery to Watermark's receiving office.

Carolyn believes that much of Watermark's success is due to members' participation as they see Watermark's success or failure as their responsibility. At their annual general meeting, they take the major decisions regarding policy and plans and elect a Board of Directors that meets every month to check on operations. A manager, appointed by the Board, runs daily operations.

As Gloria Steinem, the noted American feminist, observes: 'It's neither capitalism nor socialism, but something else. The organizational structure is more lateral than vertical, more co-operative than hierarchical, more family than pyramid. Everyone participates in this co-operative; everyone owns it. The jobs are adjusted to life needs, such as taking care of children and parents'.

Yet its social justice goals also cause problems. The time spent on helping, counselling and training might otherwise be spent on marketing. However, Watermark's growing membership and unfavourable economic conditions have necessitated a gradual shift from this individual attention to business-related activities.

There are, no doubt, many other reasons for Watermark's success. These include low capital outlay since the objects are made at home; the independence offered by a geographically advantageous location and proximity to customers; the few skills required to begin working and facilities for on-site training; a system of self-employment that allows craftspeople to base their production on orders; and the greater availability of loans from local institutions, and so forth.

'Watermark is the flagship – the largest and most successful of the women's co-operatively owned businesses', says Gloria Steinem.

Watermark has just been chosen by the Ms. Foundation to participate in the

Collaborative Fund for Women's Economic Development because, explains Marie Wilson, its President, foundations are taking a closer interest in women's economic development. The groups are no longer working in isolation but now see themselves as part of a national movement.

Before Carolyn McKecuen came along, there were craftworkers and a market but no link between them. 'Carolyn has provided that link.'

'Manos del Uruguay': craftswomen's rural textile co-operatives

by Alicia Haber

'Manos del Uruguay' is a co-operative which, since 1968, has brought together textile craftswomen from the inner areas of the country who specialize in the spinning and weaving of wool or local natural fibres such as ramie and thistle with which they make tapestries, carpets, curtains and various kinds of rugs.

'This organization has been designed to provide work for craftswomen in the inland areas and to enable them, just as I once had the chance, to train and develop their skills. It's an institution of a productive and particularly social nature', explains Rufina Romano with enthusiasm.

Rufina herself is a weaver who comes from a small village of 700 inhabitants, Egaña in Soriano province. She runs the Soriano Crafts Co-operative and has been at the head of 'Manos del Uruguay' for three years.

The social aims of the organization emphasize that family life must be preserved as a priority in order to prevent women from being cut off from their roots. The organization encourages endeavours to promote dialogue, independence, personal development, greater self-confidence and social mobility and, through self-management, opens the way for global development.

'Everything depends here on combining efforts from various sources', claims Olga de Artagaveytia, founder of the organization and now in charge of marketing.

Let us imagine 600 craftswomen who provide collective impetus for 18 autonomous co-operatives divided up into 90 groups in 40 locations. They run each co-operative like a small independent company with 12 to 20 employees.

The system also relies on a service unit in Montevideo run by professionals and administrative staff. This is where products are designed, raw materials stored, tools made and technical training provided. This unit is also responsible for selling products, setting up funding and providing assistance and training to co-operative managers and administrative staff.

This has resulted in a whole network of regional integration that fosters a harmonious dialogue between urban and rural interests with a view to bridging the gap between town and country and between the inland areas and Montevideo, which has such a profound effect on Uruguayan society. It also enables poor craftswomen to work together in a joint effort with the middle echelons of the civil service and the creators and their associates who represent the upper middle class.

'Manos del Uruguay' brings together and reconciles a wide range of vocations in order

RUFINA ROMANO,
THE TIRELESS ORGANIZER,
AT WORK WHILE MANAGING
'MANOS DEL URUGUAY'.

104

to promote a carefully devised productive, social scheme.

A feature of the organization's work and creativity has always been concern for the social dimension. In Olga's words, 'when we set up "Manos del Uruguay", the country was in the throes of a recession, rural pay was declining and production stagnating, which meant that the resources of the working population were threatened. Additional income had to be found urgently, such as that which women could bring in'.

And Rufina Romano refers to her early days in 1975 when 'I lived on a farm in the country, which had neither water nor electricity. I used to work the land with my husband and seven children. My husband was also a mechanic but what he earned just wasn't enough and there was no possibility for me to find a job locally'.

In Uruguay, job opportunities in the inland, particularly rural areas have always been limited, and unrestricted urbanization has meant that towns have developed to the detriment of the countryside (80 per cent of the population now live in urban areas, with over 45 per cent in and around Montevideo).

Accordingly, the situation is even more serious for women who find few opportunities for productive development. As they lack experience and adequate training, they have no amenities where they could envisage any profitable activity and often have to contend with opposition in the traditional family context. In some remote areas, women have still to put up with a status that is unworthy of a Europeanized country like Uruguay, with a very high literacy rate, and a predominantly urban population, dominated by the middle classes. Such women are ignored outside their role of housewife or poorly paid domestic employee and have no prospects other than marriage, child-bearing and a cloistered life at home, in relative isolation and with little autonomy.

In the 1960s when circumstances had worsened through the recession that had overtaken the country, Olga de Artagaveytia and four of her friends, the wives of prosperous landowners, devised a plan to create job opportunities in the traditional textile crafts that had always been practised in the home. In this venture, they enjoyed the support of the Uruguayan branch of the World Crafts Council.

'First of all, we conducted a sort of opinion poll to try and gather information about what experience people actually had. In parallel to the market, we began to locate the craftswomen and assess their manual skills before convincing them of how worthwhile our plan was. Finally, we brought them all together to develop the global concept of "Manos del Uruguay". Many of the craftswomen in the most remote, isolated villages and *ranchos* rose to the challenge. Little by little, with a lot of effort and perseverance, we obtained their agreement – sometimes half-hearted and mistrustful, at other times resolute and daring.'

Rufina Romano remembers what a gamble 'Manos del Uruguay' was and what it meant to her and her family: 'I had my own problem. As I had never been beyond the third form at our village school, I didn't feel up to providing my own children with guidance as I felt inferior, even in my own personality because I was shy and I found it difficult to take part in things and to communicate with others. It wasn't very easy to start with as far as my family was concerned, as I started to go out to meetings. My husband and children were used to seeing me at home all the time. I often tell my friends how, at that time, I used to sign "contracts" with my husband and our eldest children, and try to explain things very clearly so that they would understand that there was a good reason for attending the meetings. We tried together to come to terms with my new role.

'The problem was that nearly the whole village used to ask me questions as, in these inland areas, people find it difficult to accept that a woman should go out to work during regular working hours and not be at home.

'For me, the major challenge was the need to make a double effort, to have a double day to do. At the beginning, I did my spinning at night. During the day, I had the domestic chores to do as well as working in the fields. That meant an 18-hour day.'

Initially, and until the system was really operational, these women had to display a lot of tenacity in coping with the reticence of their families and the community, overcoming their own misgivings with regard to a project that struck them as utopian and enduring gruelling working days and overcoming those difficulties that are inherent in rural life (poor roads, no transport and a modest dwelling without electricity).

It all proved worthwhile subsequently. Today, 'Manos del Uruguay' can draw on what in the past was a dormant reserve of productivity and feminine expression while providing the means to solve economic and social problems.

A textile tradition safeguarded

Rufina Romano was born into this tradition and had some experience of it: 'My mother's family was of Italian origin. In my grandmother's and mother's house, we used to do spinning and weaving and I knew just one or two things about it so as to help my mum.'

'At the beginning,' Olga de Artagaveytia recalls, 'the women used to produce fairly coarse objects for domestic use, particularly ponchos, protective covers, bridles and bags for the horses, bedspreads and blankets. Whenever they sold any, it was usually to local people or according to ancient bartering methods, which did not do much to encourage their economic and professional development. Then we met a small group of more urban women, who were descended from Russian, German, Spanish and British families who used more refined European techniques, with perfect results in weaving, macramé and crochet, but whose innovation and creativity in design had become stagnant which meant that their products had become hard to sell.'

Spinning and weaving wool have always played an important part in the economy of the inland areas of Uruguay, in view of large-scale sheep-rearing, and were always practised by women (93.8 per cent) in accordance with their traditional role and ancestral customs. But their creativity was restricted for lack of any historical, popular tradition in Uruguay.

Most of the craftswomen made do with rudimentary techniques, spinning or weaving by hand or with a rustic loom or frame. One of the principal tools was the 'creole loom' dating back to the colonial period (eighteenth century) and composed of a crude wooden frame in which nails were embedded for fixing a wool warp. For weaving, coarse wool was used with a foot-operated spinning wheel and a spindle. The wool was neither washed nor dyed but if, by chance, it was, this was done with a few dyes extracted from plants which provided a limited range of ochres and greys. The design was also very simple, based on very sober plain or striped wefts.

On the way to innovation: a style and a trademark

The craftswomen responded to the initiative by starting to draw on the breadth of their own experience and know-how in the field of textiles.

106

THROUGHOUT THE COUNTRY,
RURAL WEAVING
WORKSHOPS COMPLETE
THE FIRM'S ORDERS.

'At the co-operative, I used to do the spinning', relates Rufina Romano, 'but when I was given the chance of learning how to weave, I jumped at it. To start with, I used to weave by hand and I've only been using a manual loom for the past five years. Today, I am responsible for the finishing touches performed by a group of women working on the looms. I've been able to do this, of course, after getting enough training and experience. It's a job I enjoy and which pays well.'

Like Rufina, all the women have had to acquire extra experience to raise the standards of the co-operatives. 'Manos del Uruguay' has done a lot to facilitate this upgrading which has now become permanently available. There has been a gradual process of apprenticeship which has led to the use of modern looms and craft weaving machines, more refined techniques, various dyeing methods and rigorous quality control.

'In our organization, there is a real link between craftsperson and designer. Fortunately, there is plenty of freedom of creation as there is no risk of going against tradition', as Olga explains. Given the nature of Uruguay and its limited traditions, this approach does not run counter to the ancestral heritage.

Rufina appreciates the creativity of professional designers and her experience has shown her that they tend to adapt to the process: 'There's never any clashing. As weavers, we are convinced that designers make a very positive contribution to our work and most, in fact virtually all of us, are very satisfied with the products we make. Once they are finished, we find them beautiful'.

The growing influence of designers has been very significant and they now provide substantial support to 'Manos del Uruguay', as the design component has a stimulating effect on the craftswomen as confirmed by Victoria

Varela, a professional stylist. 'The final product we create can genuinely be called a "fashion object".' What this means is that 'Manos del Uruguay' has succeeded in developing from the stage of modest, ordinary domestic handicrafts, with poor profitability and limited production that could barely satisfy family needs, making its presence felt on local and international markets alike with products that are remarkable in terms of both aesthetics and quality.

Thanks to the reputation of its trademark, it has become an export company recognized both locally and nationally for the originality of its products. It has also achieved distinction for the way it enhances rusticity and 100 per cent natural materials, the safeguarding of certain traditional methods combined with modern techniques and the use of untreated spun wool to develop its noble yet versatile features to the full. The choice of textures, the combination of materials and research into chromatic aspects on the basis of formulae that provide over 90 different shades, are all remarkable assets.

Victoria Varela sees some products as being more audacious than others such as 'a bag made of sheepskin and fleece or sweaters made of machine-spun natural-coloured wool, with the use of colouring that is specific to the various breeds of sheep. Products such as these can't be produced in an industrial context and lie strictly within the compass of craft skills'.

Various interesting creations are now available such as ponchos with an unusual texture or patchwork-decorated sweaters, combining manual and machine work. In the more imaginative vein, highly refined products with a very fine weave have also been produced by combining various techniques. A recent success story has been that of pure linen. 'Manos del Uruguay' have always chosen a sober touch and lack of ornamentation for their products in keeping with the Uruguayan character and reflecting the local identity.

Rufina Romano now has managerial responsibilities in the organization. We met her for an interview in February 1995.

Alicia Haber: How did you reach this particular position?

Rufina Romano: My career with 'Manos' has not only been that of craftswoman (although it has given me an opportunity to create quality products), but that of manager. I've always enjoyed taking a lead in things, it's something I'm good at. After joining the co-operative, I was elected to the tax committee and I embarked on further training, first in villages and then in Montevideo and subsequently abroad. In 1980, on the occasion of an exchange between co-operatives, I went to Chile and in 1987 I took part in the International Crafts Fair and attended training courses at Mondragón. In 1990, I attended the IDB Conference in Santo Domingo and in 1994 did a traineeship with a small company in Córdoba. I have been elected president of my co-operative for the fourth time and, for the last three years, I have held the Chair of the Executive Committee.

A. H.: It must be difficult to supervise productivity and maintain efficiency in this field. How do you do it?

R. R.: Well, there's the management which must be the boss and that's quite difficult for me. After all, I'm dealing with my own colleagues and, in some cases, members of my own family. Taking decisions that reflect a certain rigour is not always easy in this environment, especially as women find it difficult to see themselves as bosses. Of course, we have to maintain

productivity and quality as 'Manos' is one of the most demanding enterprises in this field.

A. H.: Rufina, tell us about an ordinary day in your life.

R. R.: Running 'Manos' is very time-consuming. I have to follow up decisions, carry out administrative tasks and negotiate with many different people. At the same time, I travel a lot in Uruguay to maintain contact with the co-operatives and to run my own group. The person in charge cannot leave all the work to others. For example, at present, I have to go to Egaña every two weeks. Tomorrow, for instance (and it's not an unusual day by any means), I have to take to the road: I have to go to my co-operative in Montevideo to bring some raw materials; there, I'll supervise the delivery of orders for dispatch and then programme the surplus for another order. Then I'll go on to Mercedes and come back to sleep at Egaña. I set off on the bus at 1.30 in the morning and get back to the village at 9.30 in the evening, having done the whole trip on public transport. But I'm pretty well organized and I always take my little pillow with me!

A. H.: What gives you the greatest satisfaction and requires the greatest sacrifice?

R. R.: You know, I had a vocation for teaching but I never had the opportunity to become a teacher. Thanks to 'Manos', I have acquired another form of education. My managerial vocation has developed and I have applied it to other means of managing the rural environment. I was in charge of the first crèche in Egaña and of 4 or 5 other similar institutions in the region after a mutual assistance plan for 67 homes was implemented. I have also taken part in education projects related to primary education. The greatest sacrifice I've had to make has undoubtedly been finding enough time for my children. It has always been a difficult choice as my two youngest daughters have had to become boarders. I feel guilty about it. Nevertheless, with time and a degree of personal success (as, after all, that sort of thing does matter), my family has come to be proud of me. My children recognize that these efforts have been worthwhile. But it's been a long haul. All too often, my husband would say: 'You're worn out, why don't you drop everything!' But I thought I was getting personal satisfaction out of it and a measure of economic independence that would help me to make plans for our family's future. So in spite of the physical exhaustion, I went on and I'm absolutely sure that I took the right decision.

A. H.: Now that you have acquired all this experience, what are your plans?

R. R.: What I want is to continue working with 'Manos del Uruguay'. I really like working in a team. I would like to pass on all that I have learned and try to motivate and give similar opportunities to other craftswomen. I want to help women in inland Uruguay to educate themselves.

I would also like to be involved with other groups of this kind, such as the 'Red de Mujeres Rurales', a new organization set up by countrywomen. We meet to exchange ideas on managerial problems and programmes. In addition to that, running 'Manos' takes up a lot of my time and attention. Nevertheless, at the age of 56, I feel really active!

A. H.: Are you still convinced of the importance of 'Manos del Uruguay' for women and its impact on Uruguay?

R. R: Of course I am! 'Manos' is an irreplaceable organization in terms of the income it brings to the inner areas of the country. At certain times and in certain places it provides the only source of income. It enables the commercial network to develop and the region to grow more active. When it comes to exports, it makes a very appreciable contribution.

In my opinion, however, it's still in the social and cultural field that it makes its greatest contribution and I must emphasize that. Unfortunately, we don't have any parameter whereby we can actually measure it.

People feel the need to do things and they want to find solutions to their problems. In the villages, for instance, many of the local committees have now come to rely on the women of 'Manos del Uruguay'. The guiding idea is that we must overcome all the obstacles.

The authors

Jasleen Dhamija (India). Has a lifetime's involvement in the development of craft, folk arts, cross-cultural exchanges and performing arts, especially in the Asia–Pacific region. Began work in India and participated in the rural programmes based on Gandhist philosophy. Has published numerous books and studies on the revival of traditional crafts. Consultant and adviser for several international organizations with which she has close working relationships. President of the Jury for the UNESCO Crafts Prize for Asia (1992) and Member of the UNESCO/ILO Committee of Experts for the Status of Artisans.

Fatoumata Agnès Diaroumeye (Niger). Director of the Multinational Programming and Operational Centre for Central Africa in Yaoundé (Cameroon). Responsible for several programmes for social planning, and activities in support of various women's projects. Has organized and participated in many meetings on these topics. Her books deal mainly with the condition of women and their role in present-day society, particularly in rural areas.

Lyda del Carmen Díaz López (Colombia). Anthropologist and museologist. Has been working for fifteen years in the socio-economic and cultural development of craft activities in Colombia. Presently in charge of the 'Artesanías de Colombia' programme for crafts promotion in the west of the country Has written a number of studies and monographs on craft techniques in different Colombian communities. Member of the Ibero-American Association for the Development and Marketing of Crafts (AIDECA).

Jocelyne Étienne-Nugue (France). Researcher, consultant and specialist in traditional and comparative traditional crafts techniques. Has been involved for many years in projects for the safeguard and adaptation of crafts in Black Africa. Has participated since 1975 in several UNESCO projects for crafts development in the world. Author of several surveys on traditional crafts in Black Africa and of a *Methodological Guide to the Collection of Data on Crafts.* Has contributed to the preparation of UNESCO's *Crafts from All the World* catalogues and exhibitions.

Alicia Haber (Uruguay). Art historian and critic. Professor of History of Art at the Instituto de Profesores in Montevideo. As a visual-arts adviser, has organized several exhibitions. Has also published numerous books and essays on the visual arts and written in the *El País* daily more than 600 articles mainly on arts and crafts in Uruguay. Has lectured in American universities on several occasions.

Hamma Hanachi (Tunisia). Journalist and art historian. Travels in the world of art, culture and tourism with his pen, ideas and deeds. Has presented radio programmes in Tunis and Brussels. Has contributed to several cultural magazines and to the culture section of the *La Presse* daily in Tunisia. Member of the Tunisian Association of Film Critics and the Tunisian Association of Journalists. Now contributes to the *L'hebdo touristique* weekly.

Mairead McAnallen (Ireland). Editor of and contributor to several magazines and catalogues on crafts and tourism. Has participated in development workshops for professional craftmakers. Director of many travelling crafts exhibitions. Editor from 1986 to 1992 of *Craft Review* magazine published by the Crafts Council of Ireland.

Tsokolo 'Muso (Lesotho). Founder and director of the Lesotho Academy of Arts. Has a wide professional experience in teaching, community development and social affairs. Has taken part in artistic activities (music and drama) in Lesotho as well as festivals abroad. A regular contributor to two weeklies commenting on the state of the visual or performing arts in Lesotho.

Caroline Ramsay (United States of America). Crafts development and marketing specialist. Has participated in the co-operation programmes of numerous international organizations and United Nations agencies in the developing countries, and is the author of articles and publications, while running a boutique selling crafts from low-income co-operatives. Founded the Crafts Center which provides assistance in the organization and sponsoring of numerous activities in the crafts sector (exhibitions, production, promotion and marketing). Editor of the *Crafts News* quarterly newsletter and a biennial *International Directory of Resources for Artisans*.

Helen Ross (Australia). Writer and Professor of Art History with a special interest in the sociology of the arts and gender issues within the art world. Comes from a craft background and has undertaken university studies in ceramics. Managed a project to take an exhibition of women's craftwork to the Fourth World Conference on Women in Beijing in September 1995.

Shalini Saran (India). Freelance journalist since 1980, having being assistant-director of a publishing house. Author of many articles and short stories. As a talented photographer, has participated in photographic exhibitions in many countries and received several awards. Her writings deal mainly with crafts, traditions, the history of India and various aspects of Islam in Indian civilization.

112